I cannot think of
churches and minis
it is a call to abandon the carnal strategies of the secular world
that have no power to convert the soul. For the solidly Reformed,
it is a call to stand and preach the gospel in the power of the Holy
Spirit and to earnestly and urgently call men to repentance and
faith. In this brief work, Jeff Smith proves that true gospel
preaching is not less than accurate exposition, but it is much
more—it is prayer, proclamation, persuasion, and pleading. This
book will wake you from the deception of pragmatism and the
comfortable slumber of orthodoxy. It will bid you stand in a
valley of dry bones and call the dead to live.

—Paul Washer
Founder, HeartCry Missionary Society

If most pastors are anything like me, they find preaching to build
up the saints far, far easier than preaching to win lost men and
women to saving faith in Christ. In his new book, *Preaching for
Conversions*, Jeff Smith provides us with a stimulating series of
chapters, all aimed at helping men preach more deliberately and
more persuasively the saving gospel of our Lord Jesus Christ.
This is not just another primer on "How to"; it is a pastor
teaching us from God's Word and from examples in church
history and, out of his own experience, the biblical pattern and
privilege of preaching evangelistically. It is a pleasure to
commend *Preaching for Conversions*.

—Ian Hamilton
Teaches historical theology at Greenville Presbyterian
Theological Seminary, South Carolina, and Westminster
Presbyterian Theological Seminary, Newcastle, England

Many who preach evangelically fail to preach evangelistically. Perhaps, sadly, we do not know quite what to do or where to begin. Without for a moment denying the sovereign majesty of a saving God, Jeffery Smith presses home the beauty, clarity and urgency of the gospel on all who are called to preach it, and underlines the necessity of cultivating a convicting and converting intent in our preaching. We are to preach for conversions, so to speak, under God, as to be his means of bringing the dead to life, those in darkness to light. This is a holy skill we need to cultivate today, and these pages will help you understand both what you are to do and how to do it.

—Jeremy Walker,
Pastor, Maidenbower Baptist Church (UK)

I see Jeff Smith as an impressive kingdom warrior—a Captain America, running among us foot soldiers. I highly respect him, his opinions, his convictions, and his ministry. When he speaks or writes, I listen. Here, he calls us to preach for conversions, to plan determined and continuous gospel assaults on the souls of lost sinners, keeping in mind that many who think they're safe for eternity are deceived by the enemy. He emboldens us to bring hurt before healing, conviction before comfort. He drives us to helpless dependence, then directs us to Almighty power. Read this, pastor! It will galvanize you to fight a better fight for your hearers and our King.

—Mark Chanski
Pastor, Harbor Church in Holland, MI
Professor of Hermeneutics at Reformed Baptist Seminary

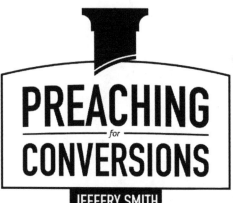

PREACHING *for* **CONVERSIONS**

JEFFERY SMITH

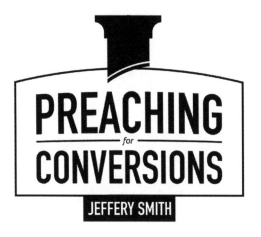

PREACHING
for
CONVERSIONS

JEFFERY SMITH

FREE GRACE PRESS

Preaching for Conversions

Free Grace Press
1076 Harkrider
Conway, AR 72032
freegracepress.com

Cover design by Brandon Scalf

ISBN: 978-1-95259-900-2

Contents

Introduction

In the fall of 2018, I delivered two messages on the subject of preaching for conversions at a conference of Reformed Baptist and Presbyterian pastors in Montville, New Jersey. Afterward, a number of my ministerial colleagues urged me to consider putting those sermons into print. After reflecting on this, I decided to accept this counsel, though expanding my consideration of the subject a bit beyond what was covered in those two sermons.

This little book does not attempt to be a work specifically on the topics of sermon preparation and delivery. I assume that most of my readers are men who know the basics of preaching or are preparing to be preachers and have access to the many excellent books on this subject.[1] Rather, my concern in these pages is to urge

---

[1] For anyone desiring some recommendations, here are the four books on sermon preparation and sermon delivery I would most highly recommend, though many other good ones are available: D. Martyn Lloyd-Jones, *Preaching & Preachers*, 40th Anniversary Edition (Grand Rapids, MI: Zondervan, 2011); C.H. Spurgeon, *Lectures to My Students, Vol. 1–3* (Pasadena, TX: Pilgrim, 1990); Al Martin, *Pastoral Theology, Vol. 2: The Man of God, His Preaching And Teaching Labors* (Montville, NJ: Trinity Pulpit, 2018), and Stuart Olyott, *Preaching Pure and Simple* (Bridgend, Wales: Bryntirion, 2007).

my colleagues in the pastoral ministry to preach for *conversions in their local church settings.* I argue for the importance of this and seek to draw out and apply from the Scriptures practical guidance for myself and my ministerial fellows regarding the best ways we may do it. It is also my concern to remove common errors and misconceptions that can sometimes hinder Reformed men in this endeavor.

Finally, I hope to encourage greater urgency about this and to stir us up to pray, and to urge our congregations to pray, for more conversions under our ministries. Surely, brothers, we should not be satisfied with no conversions or with only a few conversions here and there under our preaching. How can we be? Perhaps the Lord will use these few pages to help us.

I do not presume to present myself as a perfect model or even a good model. I grieve over the relatively small measure of fruit from my own efforts and long for a greater harvest of souls. These studies have been for my own benefit as much—or more—as for anyone else. May God use this modest work to help my fellow laborers in the gospel, to bless Christ's church, and to promote the advancement of His kingdom in the world.

> *Ye Christian heralds, go proclaim*
> *salvation through Emmanuel's Name…*

God shield you with a wall of fire,
With flaming zeal your breasts inspire,

Bid raging winds their fury cease,
And hush the tempests into peace.

And when our labors all are o'er,
then we shall meet to part no more;

Meet with the blood-bought throng to fall,
and crown our Jesus, Lord of all.[2]

All these chapters are derived from, and in some cases are expansions of, sermons first delivered orally and not with the purpose of written publication. As such, though various acknowledgments were given during their oral delivery, this material was not carefully footnoted. I have attempted to add appropriate notations insofar as able.

[2] From the hymn, "Ye, Christian Heralds, Go Proclaim," by Bourne H. Draper, 1803.

1

Are We Preaching for Conversions?

It should be one of the great concerns of every gospel minister to see sinners converted under his ministry. And though we recognize it is God alone who gives the increase, it should be our concern to sow seeds in the prescribed ways that are most likely to be used by God to that end.

What Do I Mean by Preaching for Conversions?

By *preaching for conversions*, I mean that we should preach sermons aimed at bringing sinners to Christ. I'm not referring to sermons that tack on an evangelistic application at the end, nor am I talking about those that include evangelistic applications here and there. There is certainly a place for that. There is a real sense in which *every* sermon should have an evangelistic element in it. If we preach biblical sermons, we are constantly preaching the gospel and applying the gospel in our sermons, whether we preach on the family, church order, Christian work ethic, or any other aspect of practical Christian living or Christian doctrine. People are sometimes converted under such sermons as the gospel is marbled within the message.

However, we should never preach sermons that could just as well be preached in a Jewish synagogue or an Islamic mosque with merely moral instruction and no reference to Christ and the gospel. As J. I. Packer writes, "The Puritan position was . . . that since all Scripture bears witness to Christ, and all sermons should aim to expound and apply what is in the Bible, all proper sermons would of necessity declare Christ and so be to some extent evangelistic. As Robert Bolton says, 'at least impliedly, if not directly.'" I agree with this wholeheartedly. But then he goes on to say of the Puritans, "The only difference was that some sermons aimed more narrowly and exclusively at converting sinners than others."[1]

And that is what I'm writing about in these pages—preaching that aims more narrowly and exclusively, or at least primarily, at converting sinners. As stated clearly by Charles Spurgeon, "Do not close a single sermon without addressing the ungodly, but at the same time set yourself seasons for a determined and continuous assault upon

---

[1] J. I. Packer, *A Quest for Godliness: The Puritan Vision of the Christian Life* (Wheaton, IL: Crossway, 1990), 166.

them, and proceed with all your soul to the conflict. On such occasions aim distinctly at . . . conversions."[2]

I wonder, Pastor, do you ever preach sermons like that—sermons that aim distinctly at conversions? Lately, a number of men have been sounding the alarm that there seems to be a great dearth of this kind of preaching in Reformed churches.[3] Dr. David Murray, for example, recently wrote an excellent series of blogs in which he argues this, and others have expressed this concern.[4] Of course, I'm not privy to what is preached in every Reformed church, so I can't be dogmatic about that. And it is not my purpose, necessarily, to advocate for preaching at least one sermon specifically aimed at conversions every week. D. Martyn Lloyd-Jones made that his practice, and in many of the Scottish churches, this has been the tradition. Though that may be a good idea, my concern is simply to argue that we, at least, need to be including conversion-aimed preaching in our overall preaching

---

[2] Charles Spurgeon, "On Conversion as Our Aim" in *Lectures to My Students* (Pasadena, TX: Pilgrim, 1990), 2:188.

[3] See, for example, Conrad Mbewe's article in *Banner of Truth* "Evangelistic Preaching: A Lost Art," June 22, 2005, https://bannerof truth.org/us/resources/articles/2005/evangelistic-preaching-a-lost-art and Iain H. Murray's article entitled "'Expository Preaching' — Time for Caution," June 18, 2010, https://banneroftruth.org/us/resources/articles/2010/expository-preaching-time-for-caution.

[4] David Murray, "Evangelistic Preaching," *Head, Heart, Hand* (blog) May 1, 2010, https://headhearthand.org/blog/2010/05/01/evangelistic-preaching-full-text.

ministry. I am afraid those sounding an alarm may be right. It may be that it does not happen as often as it should.

We are commanded, as ministers of the Word, to "do the work of an evangelist" (2 Tim. 4:5). Regardless of how we interpret the word "evangelist" in this text, one thing is clear: Paul is reminding Timothy that as preachers of the Word we must be preachers of the gospel (i.e., preachers of the evangel). Granted, the gospel is to be preached to those who already believe, but certainly not only to such. We've been called in the Great Commission to preach the gospel to the lost with the distinct aim of making new disciples—the aim of seeing men and women converted to faith in Jesus Christ. Are we preaching sermons with this as our objective?

Several issues may be keeping us from doing as we ought. For example, one of the hindrances to preaching for conversions is uncertainty about how to do it. This can lead to either a failure to preach evangelistically or to a neglect of some of the important facets of evangelistic preaching. This uncertainty can be increased by those of us who hold to a Reformed view of anthropology and soteriology; often there is a lack clarity on how evangelistic preaching relates to the doctrines of sovereign grace. Not only may this result in a neglect of evangelistic preaching but it can also result in evangelistic preaching that is hesitant and lacking in warmth and urgency.

But there's another hindrance. Perhaps someone says, "I'd love to preach for conversions, but if I did so in my church, I'd be preaching for conversions of people who are already converted." I think in the minds of many this is a real and serious hindrance. It could be that, in some churches, this is the main reason for a lack of sermons with conversion as the specific aim.

Of course, we have other venues for preaching evangelistically, and certainly we should not limit it to the inside of our church buildings. Perhaps this is something we all need to be challenged on. For instance, Ryan Denton and Scott Smith recently published an excellent book about open-air preaching.[5] Opportunities also abound for preaching at rescue missions or at the local jail or prison, and we can engage the lost in our communities by means of tract distribution and gospel conversations.

But for those of us who are busy pastors, I don't think we should feel guilty about the fact that our *primary* way and opportunity of doing evangelism is in our week-to-week pulpit ministry. In fact, one of my main objectives in this book is to encourage you to preach evangelistic sermons to your congregation even if you think most of your congregation is already converted.

---

[5] Ryan Denton and Scott Smith, *A Certain Sound: A Primer on Open Air Preaching* (Grand Rapids: Reformation Heritage Books, 2019).

Reasons to Preach
Evangelistically to Your Congregation

David Murray is exceptionally helpful in one of his blog posts about the reasons for preaching evangelistically to your congregation.[6] First, as Dr. Murray points out, we should preach for conversions because our people will be more encouraged to bring their lost friends to the services. If you don't have unconverted people attending your services, perhaps you should preach some evangelistic sermons until you do. What do I mean? Well, it may be that one of the reasons your folks rarely bring lost friends to the services is they know most of the preaching will be directed to Christians— and not just Christians but to well-taught Reformed Christians. They're afraid that if they bring any of their lost friends, neighbors, or family members, the messages will be too difficult for them to follow. Therefore, they don't invite them. But if they knew that every week—or at least often or at regular, stated, pre-announced times—messages will be specifically directed to the lost, it will motivate your folks to invite their unsaved friends to the services.

---

[6] David Murray, "Why preach evangelistic sermons?" *Head, Heart, Hand* (blog), April 28, 2010, http://headhearthand.org/blog/2010/04/28/why-preach-evangelistic-sermons. This paragraph is basically a summary of one of his arguments.

Second, even those who are already converted need to hear evangelistic sermons. Why? Because it's like getting converted all over again. Have you ever had one of your people come up after an evangelistic message and say, "Pastor, that was so convicting and at the same time so refreshing! It was like getting saved all over again." Our folks need to have that experience, and they need to have it often. There is a sense in which the entire Christian life is a life of continually being converted. We not only enter the narrow gate of conversion by repentance and faith in Christ, but as I believe it was Matthew Henry who said, "Repentance and faith are the two legs by which we walk the narrow road all the way to heaven." To quote Murray:

> Christians also need to hear evangelistic preaching. Why? . . . In the absence of it, Christians forget. We forget the pit we were dug out of, we forget the debt we were in, and we forget the remarkable work of God in our life. In the absence of evangelistic preaching, the memory of saving grace fades, weakens, and disappears. In its place comes proud self-confidence and self-focus, which quickly drains prayerful concern for the souls of others.

But under biblical evangelistic preaching, as he goes on to say,

> [Christians] are re-humbled, re-convicted and reminded of what they have been saved from. They re-repent, re-believe, and re-kindle their first love, . . . [and

they] become enthusiastic carriers, as they go out into the world with a renewed and prayerful vision and mission for the lost and the perishing all around them.[7]

A third reason to preach evangelistic sermons is the fact that everyone in your congregation is not converted. Children, and probably others, may not be saved, and chances are there are people who *think* they're born again but are not. When you rarely preach for conversions, the danger is that the children of the congregation may grow up assuming they're saved when they're not, and others will assume they're saved when they're not.[8] And even if there is only one person in your entire congregation who is unconverted, shouldn't you preach for that person's conversion?

Geoff Thomas tells an interesting story Edward Payson, one of the great preachers of the Second Great Awakening in America. There was once an occasion in which

Payson traveled through a violent storm to get to the church. Not long after he entered the empty building the door opened again, and another man entered for the service of worship. This man was a visitor and had come from a distance just to hear Dr. Payson preach. That was enough for the preacher to abandon any thoughts of

[7] Murray, "Why preach evangelistic sermons?"
[8] Murray.

canceling the services. Payson determined to speak, even if no one else came.[9]

At the appointed time, Payson got up and preached, though no one else showed up for the service because of the severity of the storm. It was just him and the man visiting. Sometime later, during the following year, Payson met this man again. "I enjoyed the sermon," he told Payson. He went on:

> I never heard a better one. Remember, I was sitting in the front, and whenever you said some things that were pretty hard, condemning men's sins, I'd glance around and see who you were getting at, and there was only me there! So I said to myself, "He must mean you, Pompey, you old sinner!" Dr. Payson, it was that sermon that set me thinking what a wicked man I've been, and since then I haven't missed a service at the church I attend.[10]

You see, the Lord honored Payson's faithfulness in preaching to that one man.

Now let me say something very briefly about the approach I plan to take in the remainder of this book. This is a large subject. There's a lot we could get into, but I'm determined to keep this relatively concise and, therefore, more likely to be read. What I want to do is focus on some

---

[9] Geoffrey Thomas, *Philip and the Revival in Samaria* (Carlisle, PA: Banner of Truth, 2005), 109–110.

[10] Thomas, 109–110.

key areas I think we need to be reminded of—areas I think must be underscored because they are sometimes missing notes in our preaching or are categories of emphasis preachers are not always as clear about as we should be. Then I hope to focus in the last two chapters on the role of the Holy Spirit in preaching for conversions and the vital importance of praying for conversions.

2

Preaching to
Awaken Sinners

Now in the fifteenth year of the reign of Tiberius Caesar, Pontius Pilate being governor of Judea, Herod being tetrarch of Galilee, his brother Philip tetrarch of Iturea and the region of Trachonitis, and Lysanias tetrarch of Abilene, while Annas and Caiaphas were high priests, the word of God came to John the son of Zacharias in the wilderness. And he went into all the region around the Jordan, preaching a baptism of repentance for the remission of sins, as it is written in the book of the words of Isaiah the prophet, saying: "The voice of one crying in the wilderness: 'Prepare the way of the LORD; Make His paths straight. Every valley shall be filled And every mountain and hill brought low; The crooked places shall be made straight and the rough ways smooth; And all flesh shall see the salvation of God.'" Then he said to the multitudes that came out to be baptized by him, "Brood of vipers! Who warned you to flee from the wrath to come? Therefore bear fruits worthy of repentance, and do not begin to say to yourselves, 'We have Abraham as our father.' For I say to you that God is able to raise up children to Abraham from these stones. And even now the ax is laid to the root of the trees. Therefore every tree which does not bear good fruit is cut down

*and thrown into the fire." So the people asked him, saying, "What
shall we do then?"[1] He answered and said to them, "He who has
two tunics, let him give to him who has none; and he who has
food, let him do likewise." Then tax collectors also came to be
baptized, and said to him, "Teacher, what shall we do?" And he
said to them, "Collect no more than what is appointed for you."
Likewise the soldiers asked him, saying, "And what shall we do?"
So he said to them, "Do not intimidate anyone or accuse falsely,
and be content with your wages." Now as the people were in
expectation, and all reasoned in their hearts about John, whether
he was the Christ or not, John answered, saying to all, "I indeed
baptize you with water; but One mightier than I is coming, whose
sandal strap I am not worthy to loose. He will baptize you with
the Holy Spirit and fire. His winnowing fan is in His hand, and
He will thoroughly clean out His threshing floor, and gather the
wheat into His barn; but the chaff He will burn with
unquenchable fire." And with many other exhortations he
preached to the people.*

– Luke 3:1–18

Daniel Rowland ministered in Wales during the great
evangelical awakening of the mid-to-late-eighteenth
century. He didn't travel around from place to place as
much as George Whitefield and some of the others.
Instead, he labored for many years in a little town called
Llangeitho. People would travel from every part of Wales
to hear him preach, especially during the monthly
Communion service. In *The History of the Calvinistic Methodist
Fathers of Wales* we're told:

The whole population, for an area of some fifteen miles, would attend every communion Sunday, once a month, together with crowds from the furthest extremities in the north and in the south. Often there would be more than 5,000 present. . . . The roads and streets would be full of people, but without any of the bustle and tumult of a fair. Instead, the solemnity of eternity would rest upon the multitude. No levity or joking would be heard—the young and thoughtless, those who had been drawn by the crowd, or had come to satisfy their curiosity, would feel a solemnity taking hold upon them. The fields would be full of the horses of the visitors, and some hundreds of animals would be tethered together in lines along the hedgerows.[1]

What was it that brought all these people to this little community of Llangeitho? It was the preaching of God's Word by a man full of the Holy Spirit.

This account of the ministry of Daniel Rowland reminds me of the description we're given in the New Testament of the way people reacted to the preaching of John the Baptist. In Luke 3:1–18, the passage that heads this chapter, we have this remarkable description of John's ministry and the tremendous effects it produced. Suddenly a voice is heard piercing the darkness and the deadness of

[1] John Morgan Jones and William Morgan, *The Calvinistic Methodist Fathers of Wales*, trans. John Aaron (Carlisle, PA: Banner of Truth, 2008), 1:83–84.

apostate Israel—the voice of one crying in the wilderness, "Prepare the way of the Lord." And one of the amazing things about John's preaching is the large numbers of people who flocked to hear him. Luke speaks in verse 7 of multitudes going out to hear him. Matthew tells us in Matthew 3:5, "Then Jerusalem, all Judea, and all the region around Jordan went out to him." And they not only went out to hear him, but many of them also responded humbly to his message, professing repentance and being baptized.

What was it that drew the crowds? Was it a hipster style and designer skinny jeans? No, he wore a cloak woven from camel's hair and a leather belt around his waist, economical attire often worn by peasants and used to sleep on at night. Was it a ministry strategically surrounded by an innovative marketing strategy? No, John lived a simple life with humble dress and a modest diet of locusts and wild honey. Was it the location, a suburban context with easy access, a large parking area, and an attractive, inviting meeting place? No, it was none of those things we sometimes think we must have.[2]

I mean, you think the location of your church is bad? John preached in the wilderness of the Jordan. Lenski

[2] Bryn MacPhail, "Keys to Successful Ministry: Luke 3:1–20," *MacPhail's Manuscripts*, accessed May 4, 2020, http://www.reformed theology.ca/luke3.html.

describes it as a "hot uninhabited depression, which is wild in every way and removed from all civilization."[3] This doesn't sound like an ideal place to preach, does it? The fact is there is no ideal place except that place where God has presently placed us.

Was it then, perhaps, cutting-edge technology and carefully choreographed musical performances that drew the crowds? No, it was none of that. So, what was it that drew people to the ministry of John the Baptist? It was bold, Spirit-filled, conscience-convicting, judgment-warning, Christ-exalting preaching of the Word of God.

Why have I drawn our attention to this description and to the ministry of John the Baptist? I remind you that our topic is preaching for conversions. This is what John the Baptist did. He preached for conversions. As we read in verse 3 of this passage in Luke, John came preaching a baptism of repentance for the remission of sins. Matthew describes his preaching in this way: "In those days John the Baptist came preaching in the wilderness of Judea, and saying, 'Repent, for the kingdom of heaven is at hand!'" (Matt. 3:1–2). That's just another way of saying that John preached for conversions.

Sometimes the word *repentance*, or *repent*, is used together with the word *faith*: "Repent and believe the gospel."

[3] R.C.H. Lenski, *Commentary on the N.T.: The Interpretation of St. Luke's Gospel* (Edinburgh: Hendrickson, 1998), 176.

Repentance is speaking of what we might call the negative side of a saving response to the gospel—grief over and hatred of sin, while faith is speaking of the positive side of a saving response to the gospel—turning to Christ to be delivered from sin and its guilt, punishment, and domination. But at other times, as it is here, it's used alone to refer to the whole of our turning from sin to Christ. The whole of a sinner's turning from sin to God through faith in Jesus Christ is described by this word *repentance*.

In other words, John was preaching for conversions. He called men and women to repent for the forgiveness of sins. And as we see in verses 16–17 of this passage, he preached repentance by pointing them to Christ the Savior. We are told in Acts 19:4 that "John indeed baptized with a baptism of repentance, saying to the people that they should believe on Him who would come after him, that is, on Christ Jesus." In John 1:29 we see him preaching repentance and pointing to Christ as "the Lamb of God who takes away the sin of the world." Furthermore, this believing repentance was to be publicly expressed by submitting to the waters of baptism. Though this wasn't the same as Christian baptism, it was a public and outward confession of their repentance.

Therefore, though John lived before the cross and the resurrection, his message was essentially the same message you and I are called to preach. He preached the forgiveness of sins, and he preached the necessity of repentance and faith in Christ. In fact, in verse 18, Luke describes John's preaching as preaching the gospel: "And with many other exhortations he preached to the people." The Greek word translated "preached" is a form of the word *euangelizo*, which means "to preach the good news." So it says that "with many other exhortations he preached *the gospel* to the people."

John's message was the same message as the Lord Jesus. Matthew 4:17 makes this clear: "From that time Jesus began to preach and to say, 'Repent, for the kingdom of heaven is at hand.'" And it's the same message Jesus tells us to preach. When Jesus gave the Great Commission in Luke 24:46–47, He commanded that repentance and the remission of sins are to be preached in His name.

On the day of Pentecost, after Peter preached the first sermon of the beginning of the Christian church, certain people cried out, saying, "What shall we do?" Peter answered, "Repent, and let everyone of you be baptized in the name of Jesus Christ for the remission of sins" (Acts 2:38). Again, this is essentially the same message as John the Baptist.

Likewise, this is the message of the apostle Paul, who stood on Mars Hill and declared to the men of Athens that "God . . . commands all men everywhere to repent" (Acts 17:30). And when summarizing before the Ephesian elders his preaching, in Acts 20:21, Paul said that what he preached both to the Jews and to the Gentiles was "repentance toward God and faith toward our Lord Jesus Christ."

So John preached the same message Jesus and the apostles preached and the one we are called to preach. The only difference is that we have more light concerning the glory of Christ and the redemptive work of Christ than John had because we live on this side of the cross and the resurrection. We have more light and more glory. Christ has died, Christ has risen, and the Spirit has been given, yes, but John's message and ours—repentance and faith in Jesus Christ—are essentially the same.

But the main reason I want to begin with the preaching of John the Baptist is that he provides a striking illustration of something that must be included in the course of our evangelistic preaching, something that is often missing. Namely, preaching for conversions involves seeking to awaken sinners to their lost condition. I do not intend to argue that this must be the focus of every evangelistic sermon we preach but that this should be one of the components of our overall evangelistic preaching endeavors. John the Baptist provides us with an excellent example of preaching to awaken sinners to their lost condition.

One of the truths often forgotten or neglected in evangelism and in the preaching of our day is that God ordinarily does a prior work of preparation in bringing sinners to faith in Christ. Now we must be careful here to make some important distinctions. While the two are sometimes confused, there is a clear distinction between *preparationism* and *Divine preparation*. Historically, preparationism was a Roman Catholic doctrine, though there's an Arminian form of this doctrine as well. It's the idea that if you do certain things to prepare yourself as an unregenerate person, God will then give you grace. This is a serious error and a subtle way of teaching salvation by works. You do good works and try your best, and God is somehow obligated to respond to your efforts by giving you grace and faith. This is not salvation by grace; it's salvation as the reward of your efforts. We must reject this kind of preparationism.

There is also a subtler form of preparationism we need to beware of, and this is when preparation is viewed as something *qualifying* a person to come to Christ. The idea is that you must experience a certain amount of conviction of sin, or a certain degree of fear or humiliation, before you are warranted to trust in Christ and be saved. This kind of teaching effectively sets up roadblocks in the way of sinners that actually keep them from Christ. For how will you ever know that you've experienced *enough* conviction of sin or *enough* fear and humiliation for sin? This is also a subtle form of legalism, as we can make a righteousness out of our convictions of sin as though they qualify us to be saved.

Another important distinction to be made is between the *warrant of faith*, that which makes coming in faith to Christ permissible, and the *way of faith*, the ordinary manner in which the Spirit works in bringing sinners to faith in Christ. The warrant of faith is simply the command and invitation of the gospel to believe on the Lord Jesus Christ and the promise of salvation to all who do. However, ordinarily the way the Spirit works in bringing people to faith in the gospel is a different issue. (I'll have more to say on this in chapter 6.)

We must not confuse preparationism in these various forms with the legitimate teaching of Scripture. It is God's ordinary manner to do a preparatory work in the hearts of sinners when He draws them to Christ. Another way of saying it is that ordinarily regeneration is preceded by, or coincides with, the Holy Spirit's conviction of sin. The Spirit creates in the soul a painful awareness of guilt, helplessness, and danger. God often creates a need in sinners by the preaching of the law, sin, and judgment to come—preaching about the necessity of repentance and holiness of life, "without which no one shall see the Lord" (Heb. 12:14).

Our forefathers understood this, and it shaped their evangelism and the way they preached the gospel. One of their goals in preaching was not first to build up but to tear down and to humble and awaken men and women to their need. We especially see this in those periods of great revival and spiritual awakening in church history.

Sadly, this seems to have been largely forgotten and neglected today. In much of evangelicalism, conversion has been relegated simply to repeating a little prayer or by walking up to the front of the church and responding to an altar call. Also, we find in much evangelism, and in some Christian music, that the great need of men and women is described in terms of being broken—broken victims of a sad and cruel world—and not as guilty sinners deserving divine punishment. "Jesus came to heal your brokenness" is often the emphasis—where we are broken by the difficulties of life, by our mistakes, and by what bad people have done to us, etc., and Jesus came to heal our broken lives Now, there's a wonderful element of truth in that, but this can be presented in a way that brings a subtle shift away from any focus on personal culpability and responsibility for our sinful actions and attitudes. Instead, the impression is given that we are all victims rather than sinners responsible before God for our lives.

Another danger is an imbalanced understanding of what it means to be gospel-centered and Christ-centered in our preaching. Wrong ideas about this can result in the neglect of those truths designed to convict sinners and awaken them to how lost and desperate their condition in sin really is. One finds preachers who seem to fall all over themselves to be always positive—only desiring to be affirming and encouraging. Some are very quick to pronounce people saved, even those who give no indication they've ever felt themselves lost. It's not surprising that many of these so-called converts never pan out. They either can no longer be found and have gone back to the world, or they are in the church but give no evidence their hearts and lives have been changed. There's no evidence of love for Christ and serious devotion to His will.

True evangelistic preaching confronts men with their sins and explains their dreadful state before God. Until they see this in some measure, they'll never know anything of true repentance. They'll see nothing precious in Christ that should cause them to desire Him. All our talk about the necessity of the cross, about grace, about the need of the new birth, or about forgiveness, justification, salvation, and eternal life will never move them. It won't register. It will never capture their hearts unless they are brought to an awareness of their need as lost, hell-deserving sinners.

A caution is in order here, however. We must understand and acknowledge that God does not lead every sinner to Christ in precisely the same way. There's not some standardized experience with clearly defined stages and steps that anyone who is truly converted must go through. There is great variety in the way God works in preparing and bringing men and women to faith in Christ. Some are converted suddenly and dramatically; others, in a much calmer manner. Some can pinpoint the exact time of their conversion. Others can't and can only say, "Whereas before I was blind, now I see." Some suffer great terrors. Their experience is like the Philippian jailer in Acts 16. Yet others, like Lydia in the same chapter in Acts, are converted in a very calm and almost matter-of-fact way. All we read is that the Lord opened her heart to take heed to the gospel.

Nevertheless, with variety in mind, we *can* say this: No one is truly converted without being inwardly convinced that he or she needs to be and of why he or she needs to be, and without knowing and being convinced that they can do absolutely nothing to save themselves. There is a Spirit-given awareness of sin, helplessness, and danger. People must get to the end of themselves and see they have no other hope but Jesus.

Again, many of our forefathers understood this. Let me give an example from the preaching of that great English Puritan John Flavel. The perspective he expresses was typical of earlier times. Perhaps the most well-known of Flavel's works is his book *The Method of Grace*. In great detail he lays out the manner, the method, and the ways of God's grace in the salvation of His people. It's a series of thirty-five sermons divided into six categories. One of the sections includes four sermons under the heading "Things Which Ordinarily Precede and Lead to a Coming to Christ." He addresses in those four sermons the work of God's Spirit in convincing men of their sins and their lost condition by nature. Flavel argues that under the power of Satan, sinners have a false sense of security. This false peace is bolstered by such things as natural ignorance, religious involvement, self-deceit, superficial responses to the gospel, self-evaluations biased by self-love, comparison of themselves to others who to them appear worse than themselves, and so on. "Hence," Flavel says, "it follows that the generality of the world are in the direct path to eternal ruin."[4] Then he goes on to argue that when God shows mercy to a sinner, He strips away all false confidence by awakening that sinner to their true condition. In other words, God does a work of preparation.

Martin Luther put it this way:

The law must be laid upon those that are to be justified, that they might be shut up in the prison thereof, until the righteousness of faith comes---that, when they are cast down and humbled by the law, they should fly to Christ. The Lord humbles them, not to their destruction, but to

[4] John Flavel, "The Method of Grace," in *The Works of John Flavel*, (Carlisle, PA: Banner of Truth, 1982), 2:289–291. Flavel's teaching on this subject, and that of the Puritans in general, is considered in detail in the excellent work on this subject by Joel R. Beeke and Paul M. Smalley, *Prepared By Grace For Grace: The Puritans on God's Ordinary Way of Leading Sinners to Christ* (Grand Rapids: Reformation Heritage Books, 2013). The section on Flavel is found on pp. 177–190.

their salvation. For God wounds, that he may heal again. He kills, that he may quicken again.[5]

And likewise, Charles Spurgeon stated:

> The Christian minister . . . must declare very earnestly and pointedly *the evil of sin*, which created the need of a Saviour. Let him show that sin is a breach of the law, that it necessitates punishment, and that the wrath of God is revealed against it. . . . Open up the spirituality of the law as our Lord did, and show how it is broken by evil thoughts, intents and imaginations. By this means many sinners will be pricked in their hearts. . . . The law goes first, like a needle, and draws the gospel thread after it, therefore preach concerning sin, righteousness, and judgment to come. . . . Probe the wound and touch the very quick of the soul. Spare not the sterner themes, for men must be wounded before they can be healed, and slain before they can be made alive. No man will ever put on the robe of Christ's righteousness till he is stripped of his fig leaves, nor will he wash in the fount of mercy till he perceives his filthiness.[6]

In the parable of the sower, the Lord speaks of the sower sowing his seed in four different types of soil. He tells us

---

[5] Quoted in Charles Bridges, *The Christian Ministry with An Inquiry into the Causes of its Inefficiency* (Carlisle, PA: Banner of Truth, 1997), 232–233.

[6] Charles Spurgeon, "On Conversion as Our Aim" in *Lectures to My Students*, 2:181.

that the seed represents the gospel and the four soils represent the hearts of men. Some of the seed fell on a hardened path and never sprang up. Some fell on rocky soil and sprang up very quickly; there was hope of a harvest, but because the rock underneath had never been broken up, there was no root. They quickly withered and never brought forth fruit. Some fell among weeds and thorns and therefore were choked out. But the good soil that brought forth fruit was the soil that had been plowed. This represents a heart responding to the gospel with faith and repentance. It was soil from which the rocks and the briars and thorns had been cleared. The ground was prepared to receive the good seed.

In the language of the prophet Hosea: "Break up your fallow ground for it is time to seek the LORD, till He comes and rains righteousness on you" (Hos. 10:12). "Fallow ground" is ground that has lain idle, usually overrun with weeds. It needs to be plowed and prepared to receive the seed as it is sown.

This brings us now to the preaching of John the Baptist. How does Scripture characterize John's ministry? It was a ministry of preparation—a ministry that prepared the hearts of men and women to receive Christ. In verses 4-6 of Luke 3, Luke quotes the prophet Isaiah:

The voice of one crying in the wilderness:
"Prepare the way of the LORD;

Make His paths straight.
Every valley shall be filled
And every mountain and hill brought low;
The crooked places shall be made straight
And the rough ways smooth;
And all flesh shall see the salvation of God."

Notice the language, "The voice of one crying in the wilderness: 'Prepare the way of the LORD,'" which is drawn from the custom in the ancient world when an emperor or some other important official was about to visit a city. A herald was sent before him to announce his coming and to prepare the citizens for his arrival. John the Baptist fulfilled this role with respect to Christ. And this preparation is described in very poetic and graphic language: the construction of a great highway project, making straight paths, every valley filled, every mountain and hill brought low, crooked places made straight, rough places made smooth—followed by the promise that all flesh, all peoples, shall see the salvation of the Lord. John, in his preaching, was building a highway, a highway into the hearts of sinners for Jesus Christ, the Savior and King. Granted, John's ministry was preparation for Christ in a *historical* sense, but it was also so in an *experiential* sense in the lives of those to whom he preached.

But how did he go about seeking to do that? This will be the focus of the next chapter.

3

Emphases in Awakening Preaching

Then he said to the multitudes that came out to be baptized by him, "Brood of vipers! Who warned you to flee from the wrath to come? Therefore bear fruits worthy of repentance, and do not begin to say to yourselves, 'We have Abraham as our father.' For I say to you that God is able to raise up children to Abraham from these stones. And even now the ax is laid to the root of the trees. Therefore every tree which does not bear good fruit is cut down and thrown into the fire."

So the people asked him, saying, "What shall we do then?"

He answered and said to them, "He who has two tunics, let him give to him who has none; and he who has food, let him do likewise."

Then tax collectors also came to be baptized, and said to him, "Teacher, what shall we do?"

And he said to them, "Collect no more than what is appointed for you."

Likewise the soldiers asked him, saying, "And what shall we do?"

So he said to them, "Do not intimidate anyone or accuse falsely, and be content with your wages."

Now as the people were in expectation, and all reasoned in their hearts about John, whether he was the Christ or not, John answered, saying to all, "I indeed baptize you with water; but One mightier than I is coming, whose sandal strap I am not worthy to loose. He will baptize you with the Holy Spirit and fire. His winnowing fan is in His hand, and He will thoroughly clean out His threshing floor, and gather the wheat into His barn; but the chaff He will burn with unquenchable fire."

And with many other exhortations he preached to the people.

– Luke 3:7–18

In the last chapter, we considered the place of preparation in evangelistic preaching and saw how John the Baptist is a great example for us in this. Our concern in this chapter is looking at some of the points of emphasis in his preaching.

John Sought to Expose and Confront the Sinfulness of His Hearers

John preached against sin, and he sought to show people their sins. This is clear on the surface of this passage in Luke 3, and it's implied in the fact that he preached repentance. Calling men to repent and to turn from their sins involves showing them their sins: preaching the law, exposing sin, seeking to help people to see and honestly face their sinful state and condition.

In verses 11–14 we have examples of John getting very specific. He puts his finger directly on certain sins the people were guilty of—the people in general first; next, the tax collectors; then, the soldiers. He didn't preach to the choir. He didn't preach against all the idols of the heathen out there somewhere, the Gentile dogs, the abortionists, the transgenders, and so on, while everyone said, "Amen." He confronted those sins that tended to characterize his hearers—the greed of the people, the cheating and dishonesty of the tax collectors, the bullying tactics and discontented complaining of the soldiers. He was specific in his applications.

Faithful preaching for conversions must include this element of preaching the law and exposing sin. Man, by nature in his self-love, does not like to think of himself as a hell-deserving sinner. The heart of man is very adept at constructing protective walls of excuses and self-justifications around the conscience. Our hearts are willfully ignorant of the true nature of sin and blinded to our true condition. Therefore, part of a faithful preacher's task is to seek to break through this blindness in the effort to open the sinner's eyes to his sinfulness and danger. Of course, only the Holy Spirit can do that, but ordinarily when He does it, He does it through means. And preaching that exposes sin and seeks to show people their true condition is one of those means.

Most people are willing to admit they're not perfect and that they sin sometimes. But they also believe that, on the whole, they're good people. They tend to reason, saying to themselves, "With all the really bad, wicked people in the world—the Hitlers, the rapists and murderers, and those who still use plastic straws and eat processed foods, and so on—certainly if there is any fairness with God at all I'll be okay. Surely, He'll let people like me who are good—in comparison to other really bad people—into heaven." They compare themselves to others, contrasting their good deeds to other people's bad deeds. But they also compare their own good deeds to their own bad deeds; they have a kind of scale in their minds with their good deeds on one end of the scale and their bad deeds on the other. Since, in their opinion, their good deeds outweigh their bad deeds, they think they're okay. Therefore, we must show them that the standard by which God judges us is not by other people or their own opinion of what is good or bad. God's standard is His holy law.

We must also show them that sin is not just a matter of actions. God will hold you accountable for every word you've ever spoken, including every word of gossip, every unkind word, every time you've tried to make yourself look better by putting someone else down, every time you've fudged the truth, every lie.

We must also teach them the spirituality of the law, that the law extends to the secret thoughts and attitudes of your heart that no one sees but you. God sees them. He sees every secret thought of lust, envy, anger, pride, greed, selfishness, and impurity.

And finally, we must help them to see the gravity of their sins. Folks will often admit they sin, but they do not see the seriousness and the evil of their sins. How do you measure the seriousness of sin? The gravity of sin is partly measured by the worthiness and importance of the being we sin against. Let's say you have a pet dog that you love, and I come over to visit you at your house. While I'm there, I spit on your dog and kick it. Would that deserve punishment? Would you feel that I ought to be punished for that? Perhaps you would, perhaps not. But what if I came over to your house and, completely unprovoked, I kicked your mother and spat in her face? Or what if *you* kicked your mother and spat in her face? I think you will agree that this would be a much more serious wrong. Why? Why do we have this inherent sense that such behavior is much more heinous than hitting your dog? Is it not because your mother is much more valuable than a dog and much more worthy and deserving of your respect? She's a human being created in the image of God and the one who gave birth to you and has taken care of you.

But now let's climb up the scale of being, as it were. What do sins against God deserve? How great is God's value? How worthy is God of our respect and love? How great is our dependence on Him and our obligation to honor and obey Him? He is a being of infinite value and worth. Our obligation to Him is beyond measure. He is your Creator, who keeps you breathing and your heart beating this very moment. Is this not one reason Scripture teaches that when it comes to sins against God, justice demands an eternal punishment?[1]

Our preaching should also show people that apart from union with Christ, *all they ever do is sin.* The Bible says, "There is none who does good, no, not one" (Rom. 3:12). "How can that be?" someone asks. "Wait a minute, I've done a lot of good things. And I know people who make no claims of being Christian who do good things." Yes, in one sense, some things they do are good, and it's also true that there are degrees of wickedness. All are not as bad as they can possibly be, and there is, indeed, a kind of good that men do, even unregenerate men. When an adult child takes care of their aging parent or a person brings a meal to a neighbor who has had a death in the family, these are good things. When a father works hard to provide for his children or children are kind to their mother or when a soldier heroically throws himself on a land mine to protect

---

[1] I do not think the illustration used in this paragraph is original with me, however I don't remember for sure where I first heard it. I also used it in my book, *The Rich Man and Lazarus: The Plain Truth About Life After Death* (Durham, UK: Evangelical Press, 2019), 78.

his platoon, these are all good things in the realm of human relations. We should encourage these kinds of things and show our appreciation for them when people do them.[2]

At the same time, none of these things are truly good in a way that pleases God if we are not in Christ. In fact, they're wholly defiled and corrupted by sin. Why is that? Because there's a fundamental flaw in even the best deeds that any natural man does. Most importantly, sin is a condition of the heart. And it's a condition of the heart particularly with reference to your relationship to the God who made you. You see, there's the whole matter of your attitude toward God and your relationship to God. And as long as you are not right with God, none of your good deeds are truly pleasing to Him. They are the good deeds of a rebel.

The great nineteenth-century Baptist theologian and preacher Andrew Fuller once illustrated this by comparing men in their natural state to a band of sailors who have mutinied against their officers.[3] They put their officers in chains and take command of the ship for themselves. Imagine that on the ship these mutineers have a strict moral code. They don't lie to one another or steal from

[2] Edward Donnelly, "Genesis2 10 Total depravity," (a sermon on Genesis 6:5), SermonAudio.com, March 19, 2000, https://www.sermonaudio.com/sermoninfo.asp?SID=570910234310.

[3] Andrew Fuller, *The Complete Works of the Rev. Andrew Fuller,* rev. by Joseph Belcher (Harrisonburg, VA: Sprinkle, 1988), 2:673.

each other, and they take care of one another, sacrifice for one another, and perhaps even have religious services. Even though they do many things in their relationships to one another that might, in one sense, be called good, there is this flaw in all their goodness. All their "goodness" is, in fact, but so many self-serving expedients by which they maintain themselves in their lives of mutiny against their rightful officers. In this sense their goodness is not really good. It's defiled and corrupted. So it is with everyone who is not reconciled to God through faith in Jesus Christ. All their righteousness is corrupted and defiled and cannot save them. We must help men to see this.

An even better illustration is one I once heard in a sermon by Edward Donnelly.[4] He describes a husband who comes home from work with an expensive and beautiful bouquet of flowers for his wife in remembrance of their anniversary. She places them in a vase in the living room, and every day whenever she looks at those flowers she smiles and feels joyful inside, as they remind her of her husband's love for her. But another husband does the same thing for his wife on their anniversary. These flowers are also placed in a vase in the living room. But every time this wife walks by and sees those flowers, she is grieved and even angry on the inside. Why? What's the difference? There's no difference in the act. Both husbands did the

[4] Donnelly, "Genesis2 10 Total depravity."

same thing for their wives. So why is the one wife so sad and even angry when she looks at the flowers her husband gave her? Because, unknown to him, this wife has discovered that he is having an affair with another woman. Yes, he gave her a beautiful, large, expensive bouquet of flowers. But she knows that it's all just part of an attempt to deceive her, to make her think that all is well and that he truly loves her when he really doesn't. He loves another woman. Both husbands gave the same gift to their wives—flowers on their anniversary—but their motivations for doing it were entirely different. One of those husbands didn't do it because he sincerely loved his wife, while the other did.

In our preaching we must help people to see that it's not enough to look merely at actions. There is the whole matter of the reasons and motivation for those actions, as well as our attitude toward God and our relationship to Him. For a work to be a truly good and holy work, it must involve at least three things: It must proceed from a right heart, have a right end in view, and be according to a right rule.[5]

First, it must proceed from a right heart. A right heart is a believing heart that loves and treasures God above all things. Hebrews 11:6: "But without faith it is impossible to please [God]." And what did Jesus say is the Great

[5] Donnelly, "Genesis2 10 Total depravity."

Commandment on which all the others hang? "You shall love the Lord your God with all your heart, with all your soul, and with all your mind." Anything less than that is sin. There must be a right heart.

Also, there must also be a right end in view. There's the whole question of why a person does what they do—the motives of the heart. A person may have in view many legitimate ends in anything he or she does. There are many motives to which even the Word of God appeals. But the ultimate and essential motive that must underlie everything we do is the desire to glorify God and to enjoy Him. The Shorter Catechism says it well in answer to the question, "What is the chief end of man?" The answer, "Man's chief end is to glorify God and to enjoy Him forever." We were created to bring glory to God and to enjoy and to treasure the glory and beauty of who He is and all that He has made and all that He does in the totality of life. True goodness flows from a right heart, with a right end in view.

Thirdly, it must be in conformity to a right rule. And the only right rule is not human opinion but God's Word, by which He expresses His will for His creatures.

We have to show people that when anything a man does by nature is viewed in light of these standards—a right heart, a right motive, and a right rule—there is the total absence of any goodness in man acceptable to God.

Even your best virtues are nothing but splendid sins in God's sight. That's why we read in Proverbs 21:4, "The plowing of the wicked [is] sin." There's a sense in which you never do anything else but sin because even your best deeds are done without any genuine respect to God's glory and without any real love for the true God as revealed in the Bible.

This is the first characteristic of John's preaching for conversions. He sought to expose the sinful condition of his hearers.

John Warned People of the Wrath of God and the Judgment to Come

Second, in verse 7 of Luke 3, "Then he said to the multitudes that came out to be baptized by him, 'Brood of vipers! Who warned you to flee from the wrath to come?'" He warned about the wrath to come. "And even now the ax is laid to the root of the trees. Therefore, every tree which does not bear good fruit is cut down and thrown into the fire" (v. 9). John warned his hearers that the ax of God's judgment was about to fall upon them and if they did not repent and bring forth fruits of repentance, they would be thrown into the fire. Fire throughout the New Testament is used as a symbol for God's eternal wrath that will be poured out upon unrepentant sinners in hell. Look at verse 17, where he's warning them about it again: "His winnowing fan is in His hand, and He will thoroughly clean out His threshing floor, and gather the wheat into His barn; but the chaff He will burn with unquenchable fire." Unquenchable fire! This is the kind of language used by the Lord Jesus Himself to describe eternal hell. The fire of hell is unquenchable. There's no end; the fuel of hell's fire is never exhausted, for the sufferings of the damned will be eternal.

Now, did John preach these things because he was mean and sadistic and found pleasure in scaring people? No, he preached them because they are true and because he wanted these people to be saved from this dreadful end. Any man who truly believes the Bible and, therefore, believes what the Bible says about hell and what Jesus Himself says about hell cannot help but preach about it and warn people about it. If you never do, it's doubtful you really believe it.

Notice that John is clear in his preaching about this. C. S. Lewis tells about hearing a young man end a sermon on judgment by warning his hearers that those who do not turn to Christ will suffer "grave eschatological ramifications." After the service, Lewis asked him whether he meant that these people would go to hell. "Precisely," the preacher replied. "Then say so," Lewis said.[6] By way

---

[6] This is a common anecdote. I did not record and could not find where I first read it.

of contrast, John had no interest in muddying up what he meant with sophisticated words. He spoke plainly. When it comes to preaching for conversions, this is what we must do too. We must tell the truth, the whole truth, including *this* truth that all who die without Christ will be damned to hell for eternity.

Now we must never preach about hell without grief in our hearts and compassion for those to whom we preach. I'm sure John's heart was broken and burdened for these people. That's why he preached with such urgency and passion. I read a story recently about Francis Schaeffer. It was originally told to the person telling it by someone who visited Schaeffer and his wife Edith at L'Abri in Switzerland. There were others there and, "after dinner one night the conversation ranged over a number of profound theological issues, but suddenly someone asked Dr. Schaeffer, 'What will happen to those who have never heard of Christ?' Everyone around the dinner table waited for a great theological discourse, for this theologian to deliver a weighty intellectual answer—but none came. Instead, at the dinner table, Schaeffer bowed his head, and he wept."[7]

[7] David Legge, "Preaching Evangelistically Part 2 - The Preacher," Preach the Word, October 2010, https://www.preachtheword.com/sermon/misc0096 preacher.shtml.

Oh, that God would give us tears and cause us to weep over lost sinners. We should have tears in our eyes or, at the very least, tender compassion in our hearts and in our manner whenever we speak about hell. But at the same time, the most loving thing we can do for anyone who is outside of Christ is to tell them the truth. And the truth is that as long as they remain unconverted, they're in great danger. They are one breath, one heartbeat away, from eternal hell.

John sought to convince men of their sinful condition. He warned them about the wrath to come.

John Sought to Expose False and Self-Deceptive Hopes

Third, John knew what we must also know. He knew that when sinners are in some measure awakened to their sins and seeking relief for their consciences and from their fears, they can easily settle for something less than true conversion. They promise themselves to do better in the future. They make a few surface changes in their behavior. They say a prayer. Perhaps they start going to church or reading the Bible and doing nice things. And now they feel much better about themselves. They can easily put their trust in something other than Christ alone. They can settle for something less than a thoroughgoing conversion and deceive themselves that all is well with their soul when it's not. John was faithful to the souls of these people by seeking to expose false and deceptive hopes. We see him doing this in at least three ways in this passage.

John Warned People of Merely Trusting in Religious Ritual or Religious Activity

Though John baptized those who professed repentance, he wanted to make sure they didn't think the mere act of being baptized saved them. You can have the symbol and do the ritual without having the reality it symbolizes. Notice again the language of Luke 3:7: "Then he said to the multitudes that came out to be baptized by him." So, multitudes of folks are coming to John to be baptized. And what does John say? He doesn't just say, "All right, anyone who wants to be baptized just come on up, and we'll baptize you right now. Let's see, we had fifty decisions for Christ tonight." No, he said, "Brood of vipers! Who warned you to flee from the wrath to come? Therefore bear fruits worthy of repentance" (vv. 7–8). Wow, those are strong words, shocking words. What was he saying? He's telling them, "It's not enough to slither out of your holes"—like scared snakes were known to do in that region when fleeing from a desert brushfire—"running to me scared, thinking that baptism will make you safe. The question is, Have you truly repented? Do you have the reality the ritual symbolizes?"

This is a common problem, isn't it? Many people are trusting in the fact that they were christened or baptized as a baby or that they went to confirmation class or that they took Communion or went to confession. Even in evangelical churches, many people trust in their involvement in the church. They attend church services; perhaps they've attended church for a great many years. Or maybe they just started going to church in recent months and now they feel much better about themselves. They think, "I'm going to church now, so everything is fine. Some of my best friends are in the church." Perhaps much of their lives revolves around church and the people they know at church, so they find it hard to believe that they could be so involved with the people of God and the things of God and not be a part of God's family. This is what gives them a feeling of peace. But if that's what they're trusting in, it's a false peace, and we need to show them that.

Donald Whitney gives an illustration that is absolutely horrifying:

A member of a parachute club volunteered to videotape as a participant a jump made by the club. He leaped first, then turned the lens on the others. They floated together and finally joined hands to complete the free-falling circle. Then he taped them, one by one, as they pulled their rip cords and were jerked upright. Suddenly the image blurred as the camera swung wildly about. That was the moment the cameraman discovered he had forgotten his parachute. He had been so intent on preparing the camera and planning the filming that he overlooked his greatest priority. Although he was as active up there as anyone else in the club and enjoyed the "fellowship," he did not realize until it was too late that he was not in the same condition as the others.[8]

He was missing the one thing most needful. This is the danger, you see. A person can go to church, be involved in church and in the lives of God's people, and participate in churchly rituals and still not be one of God's people himself. John warned his hearers of merely trusting in religious ritual or religious activity. We must do the same.

John Warned His Hearers Not to Trust in Their Religious Heritage and Family Connections

Verse 8 says, "Therefore bear fruits worthy of repentance, and do not say to yourselves, 'We have Abraham as our father.' For I say to you that God is able to raise up children to Abraham from these stones." This was a great problem with many of the Jews in those days. They thought that because they had the wonderful privilege of being the physical descendants of Abraham, they were safe. They

---

[8] Donald Whitney, *How Can I Be Sure I'm a Christian?* (Colorado Springs: NavPress, 1994), 117–118.

didn't need to be born again. They didn't need to repent. They didn't need to be converted. They thought to themselves, *Gentiles may need to repent, but not us. All is well because we're the children of Abraham.* But many of them failed to realize that physical connections to Abraham, though a great privilege, were not sufficient. It is the *spiritual* children of Abraham who will be saved. As Paul writes in Romans 9:8, "Those who are the children of the flesh, these are not the children of God; but the children of the promise are counted as the seed." Or in Galatians 3:29, "And if you are Christ's, then you are Abraham's seed, and heirs according to the promise." Those who share the faith of Abraham, whether they be Jew or Gentile, are the children of God.

Something similar to this happens today as well. People will say, "My dad is a Christian," or "My mom's a Christian," or "I've gone to church as long as I can remember. I was raised in a Christian home and brought up having family devotions. I've learned the catechism, and I know all the right answers and all the right words. It's been a way of life for me as far back as I can remember." These are wonderful privileges. It's a great blessing from God to grow up in a Christian family. But again, there is this danger, and we must help our hearers to see that none of these things in themselves make you right with God. You must be born again. You must have personal dealings with Jesus Christ for yourself. You must believe in Him for yourself, repenting of your sins and taking up the cross to follow Him.

But there's a third common source of self-deception John addresses in his preaching.

John Challenged His Hearers
Not to Rely on an Empty Profession of Faith

John the Baptist challenged them not to rely on a profession of faith in Christ and repentance that had not actually produced a changed life of devotion and obedience to Christ. Again, at the end of verse 7 and beginning of verse 8 he says, "Who warned you to flee from the wrath to come? Therefore, bear fruits worthy of repentance." In other words, "You're coming to be baptized by me, professing repentance, but remember that repentance, if it's real, will show itself. It will bear fruits worthy of repentance." Verse 9 says, "Therefore every tree which does not bear good fruit is cut down and thrown into the fire." We see this emphasis again in verses 10–14. When the people came to John, asking, "What shall we do?" John put his finger on some of the specific sins they were guilty of, and he said, in essence, "If your professed repentance is real, then show it. Prove it. Stop doing this, and start doing that. Forsake your darling sin, and start practicing the opposite virtues. Prove your repentance by your obedience because talk is cheap." True conversion will always show itself in a changed life, a life marked by the serious purpose and endeavor to walk in the way of God's commandments. This is still just as true today. A profession of faith in Christ where there is no fruit of obedience to Christ is a false profession.

Now we must always make it crystal clear in our preaching that we don't become Christians on the basis of trying to obey Christ. Our obedience does not merit salvation. Salvation is by grace alone through faith. Christ, with all His saving accomplishments, is a free gift of God extended to sinners to be received by faith alone. But at the same time, where this faith exists, uniting the soul to Christ, it's always inseparable from repentance, and it brings forth the fruit of a new life of pursuing obedience. Christ doesn't save us *to* sin, He saves us *from* sin—its guilt, its punishment, but also its domination over our lives. That's why you can't separate saving faith and repentance. You can't be trusting Christ to save you from sin while still determined to keep your sin. Wherever there is true conversion, there will be fruit—the fruit of obedience.

This was not only the message of John, this was the message of Jesus Himself. It was Jesus who said, "You can know a tree by its fruits." It was Jesus who said in Matthew 7:21, "Not everyone who says to me, 'Lord, Lord,' shall enter the kingdom of heaven, but he who does the will of My Father in heaven." It is the same message preached by

John, and it is a message that still needs to be preached today.

In our efforts to awaken sinners to their lost condition, we need to show them the nature that change of life, purpose, and direction true conversion to Christ produces. We need to show them the marks and evidences of a regenerate person. I, for one, am very thankful for this kind of preaching. For many years I was a self-deceived church member and professing Christian. One of the things God used to begin to awaken me to my true condition was a book of sermons by D. Martyn Lloyd-Jones on the Sermon on the Mount that a friend had given to me as a gift. One evening while at my parents' home alone, I picked it up, and in God's kind providence, the portion I turned to and read contained three sermons on Matthew 7:21–23 entitled "False Peace," "Signs of Self Deception," and "Unconscious Hypocrisy."[9] Those sermons are great examples of preaching that address this danger of relying on a profession of faith in Christ that does not evidence itself in a changed life of devotion to Christ.

John the Baptist preached for conversions. In John we have a model, an example, of this important aspect of evangelistic preaching—preaching to awaken sinners to their need. Not that we must preach on any, or every one,

---

[9] D. Martyn Lloyd-Jones, *The Sermon on the Mount* (Grand Rapids: Eerdmans, 1996), 261–293.

of these points in every evangelistic sermon. There is a
need for balance. Too much preaching on awakening
themes like these can dishearten and discourage the
sensitive sheep among God's people, the little lambs of the
flock. It can even drive the unconverted into complete
despair. There is a right kind of despair we want them to
come to, a despair of their own righteousness and of their
own strength to save themselves. But there is also a wrong
kind of despair. We don't want them to despair of God's
mercy in Jesus Christ.

There is an interesting story about Daniel Rowland,
one of the great preachers mightily used of God in the
eighteenth-century awakening in Wales. For about five
years he powerfully preached the law as an awakened man
who himself was still unclear about the gospel of Christ,
and lacking assurance. His hearers were under terrible
spiritual distress and conviction of sin. But a Mr. Pugh
from a nearby town eventually came to him and said,
"Dear Mr. Rowland, preach the gospel to the people.
Apply the balm to their spiritual wounds and show them
the necessity of faith in the crucified Saviour." Rowland
said, "I fear that I do not have that faith, in its full active
strength myself." Mr. Pugh answered, "Preach it until you

feel you have it. If you continue to preach the law in this way, you'll kill half the population."[10]

There must be balance. We must know the people to whom we are preaching. I've been a pastor in three different congregations, and the kind of emphasis most needed has not been the same in any one of them. My first church, which I pastored for only around three and half years, was a church with many nominal professors who gave little evidence of conversion and yet believed they were headed for heaven. The congregation of the second, a church plant, where I labored for over fifteen years, was made up mostly of folks who gave much evidence of being true, sensitive-hearted Christians. The church where I have now served for roughly the last ten years has many of that description as well, but it is also in a highly populated area from which we have many visitors every Lord's Day, some of whom seem to know little of even the basic message of the gospel. We need to pray for discernment to tailor our message to the context.

But with all those qualifications, these points of emphasis we see in John ought to serve, at various times and in various ways, as themes, or components, of our overall evangelistic preaching efforts. John sought to convince men of their sinful condition before God. He

---

[10] John Morgan Jones and William Morgan, *The Calvinistic Methodist Fathers of Wales* (Edinburgh: Banner of Truth, 2008), 1:70–71.

warned them about the wrath of God against sinners and
of the judgment to come, and he sought to expose their
false and deceptive hopes.

But, praise God, that's not all John did, and that's not
all we should do when preaching for conversions. John also
proclaimed and exalted Jesus Christ as mighty to save. (I
will comment more on this in the next chapter.) We learn
in John 1:29 that John pointed sinners to Christ, saying,
"Behold! The Lamb of God, who takes away the sin of the
world!" We read in Acts 19:4 that "John . . . baptized with
a baptism of repentance, saying to the people that they
should believe on Him who would come after him, that is,
on Christ Jesus."

And then here in our text in Luke, in verse 16, he
preached Christ as the one who baptizes sinners with the
Holy Spirit, essentially saying, "Folks, I can baptize you
with water, but I can't save you. I can expose your sins, but
I have no power to free you from their guilt and from the
judgment to come. I can declare to you the necessity of
repentance, but I can't give you a new heart and the power
to do it. But I point you to one who can, the Lord Jesus
Christ! Behold, the Lamb of God, who takes away sin by
the atoning death that He will die, the one who can give
you the gift of the Holy Spirit to indwell you and enable
you to live this new life of repentance to which I'm calling
you."

That's the message John preached, and it is the message we must preach. John preached for conversions. But the main thing I want us to see in this and the preceding chapter from John's example is that preaching for conversions involves seeking to awaken sinners to their lost condition and need.

4

Preaching the
Essential Content
of the Gospel Message

Then Peter opened his mouth and said: "In truth I perceive that God shows no partiality. But in every nation whoever fears Him and works righteousness is accepted by Him. The word which God sent to the children of Israel, preaching peace through Jesus Christ—He is Lord of all— that word you know, which was proclaimed throughout all Judea, and began from Galilee after the baptism which John preached: how God anointed Jesus of Nazareth with the Holy Spirit and with power, who went about doing good and healing all who were oppressed by the devil, for God was with Him. And we are witnesses of all things which He did both in the land of the Jews and in Jerusalem, whom they killed by hanging on a tree. Him God raised up on the third day, and showed Him openly, not to all the people, but to witnesses chosen before by God, even to us who ate and drank with Him after He arose from the dead. And He commanded us to preach to the people, and to testify that it is He who was ordained by God to be Judge of the living and the dead. To Him all the prophets witness that, through His name, whoever believes in Him will receive remission of sins."

While Peter was still speaking these words, the Holy Spirit fell upon all those who heard the word.

– Acts 10:34–44

In the previous chapter we focused on the preaching of John the Baptist. John was a man who preached for conversions. Our focus was primarily to show how his preaching provides an example of one important aspect of evangelistic preaching: seeking to awaken sinners to their lost condition. But I also touched briefly on the fact that this was not all John did. John also pointed sinners to Christ the Savior. This leads us to another crucial emphasis that should mark our evangelistic preaching: declaring and explaining to men the essential content of the gospel message.

We could look further at how John the Baptist did this. But of course, John lived before the cross and the resurrection. Though his message was essentially the same as the message we are to preach, it was only in accordance with the flickering light of the early dawning of the new day. We now live under the full blazing sun of an accomplished redemption. Therefore, to get a fuller picture of what it means to preach the essential content of the gospel message, it is better to look at some of the examples we're given in the book of Acts. Luke gives us several summaries in Acts of the great evangelistic sermons preached by the apostles Peter and Paul. One approach we could take is to survey each of those sermons and draw out the common points of emphasis we see.

Instead, I've decided to focus on one of the evangelistic messages in the book of Acts, one I think that really hits, in short compass, on all the major points you'll find in each one of them. There are slight differences depending on the nature of the audience. For example, there are differences in points of contact and approach when preaching to Jews, to Gentile God-fearers, or as Paul did in Athens, to pagans. But still, in every evangelistic message summarized for us at some length in the book of Acts, the core message is the same. Certain common denominators, in almost every evangelistic message Luke records for us. In fact, this is, no doubt, one of Luke's purposes in providing these summaries of the evangelistic sermons of the apostles. He desires to make clear what the apostolic gospel is we are to believe and to preach. Again, I've chosen to focus on just one of the examples we're given, Peter's message to the people gathered in the house of Cornelius.

If you have been a Christian for more than a brief time or have read your Bible often, you're probably familiar with the context of the passage with which this chapter began, Acts 10:34–44. Here we have one of the great turning points in early church history, the beginning of the gospel being taken to the Gentiles. After Peter is given a vision, he travels to Caesarea to the house of Cornelius. When he gets there, what does he find? He finds a room full of Gentiles waiting for him and ready to hear God's Word. We read in Acts 10:24, "And the following day they entered Caesarea. Now Cornelius was waiting for them, and had called together his relatives and close friends." At the end of verse 33, Cornelius says, "We are all present before God, to hear all the things commanded you by God."

This raises a question. If you had a room full of lost people sitting before you, desiring to hear the gospel and to know the way of salvation, what would you say to them? Here's your opportunity. There they sit willing and eager to hear whatever you have to say. What would you say?

This question occurred to me when I was studying this passage, Wouldn't it be tragic if there are folks attending our churches and yet they never learn from our preaching the essential points of the gospel message? They hear various sermons on how to have a happy marriage and on child-rearing and on practical how-to Christian living and on this doctrine and that doctrine, all of which are essential. And, perhaps, they hear little snippets here and there of gospel truth. But it's never really made plain to them who Jesus is and what exactly He has done for sinners and how that relates to their situation and how they may know and have assurance of forgiveness and acceptance with God. Wouldn't that be tragic? Peter has a captive audience. What does he tell them? I don't mean to imply that we should take Peter's message and simply repeat what he says in exactly the way he said it, any more than we should do that with John's preaching. But here we have a summary of those fundamental points of emphasis that make up the essential content of the gospel message.

Peter begins with something of a preface in verses 34–35 to prepare the way. Here is the message we will focus on; verse 36 says, "The word which God sent to the children of Israel, preaching peace." This could be translated "preaching good news of peace" or "preaching the gospel of peace." The word translated "preaching" is a form of the Greek word, *euangelizo*, to announce glad tidings. We could break down Peter's gospel message in various ways, but to help us think our way through it, I have three headings.

1. The Person of the Gospel

This sermon has several points, but at the same time it has only one point: Jesus Christ. It's all about Jesus Christ. The message of the gospel centers on Christ. Did you notice that reading through it? What message is it the Holy Spirit blesses to the conversion of sinners? In a nutshell, it's the message of Christ. Indeed, this is the primary mission of the Holy Spirit. It's the peculiar ministry and business of the Holy Spirit to magnify and draw attention to the person of Jesus Christ. Do you remember what Jesus said in John 16:14 when He was speaking of the coming of the Holy Spirit? He said, "He will glorify Me." The Holy Spirit was sent, among other things, and above everything else, to glorify the Son. "For He shall not speak of Himself . . . He shall glorify Me." So Peter's message is a message that proclaims and exalts the glorious living person of the Lord Jesus Christ. He tells his hearers who Jesus is, and this is one of the things we must do in our preaching. Notice some of the ways he does this in this sermon.

Peter describes Him as the one sent by God on a mission of peace between God and sinners: "The word which God sent to the children of Israel, preaching peace through Jesus Christ" (v. 36). Peter declares that it is God who has taken the initiative to provide salvation for sinners. The same God against whom we have sinned, the same God whose wrath we deserve and are exposed to, that same God has taken the initiative in His love and mercy to provide a way in which there can be peace between Himself and the sinner. And that way is through Jesus Christ. Jesus Christ, God the Son, was *sent* into the world. He was *born* into the world of the virgin Mary, yes. But he didn't begin to exist when He was born. He was sent! He was sent from another world to make peace between God and sinners. John 3:17: "For God did not send His Son into the world to condemn the world, but that the world through Him might be saved."

Peter declares that this Jesus, the Christ, is Lord of all. "The word which God sent to the children of Israel preaching peace through Jesus Christ—He is Lord of all" (v. 36). When God undertook to make peace with rebel sinners, He didn't send a mere man. He didn't even send an angel—not even an archangel like Gabriel was sufficient for the task. He sent this One who is "Lord of all," God the Son, co-equal to the Father. He was always Lord of the universe from eternity in terms of His divine nature as God the Son. And He is now exalted as Lord of all in His human nature, joined to the divine. He is Lord of *all*, Peter says. He is Lord of all creation. He is not only Lord of the Jews but Lord of the Gentiles as well. Indeed, He is Lord of all the angels, of all principalities and powers in heavenly places. He is Lord of lords and King of kings, the sovereign King of the universe. So, Peter proclaims the person of the gospel; he explains who Jesus is.

2. The Historical Facts of the Gospel

I use the word *facts* here very deliberately. Peter preaches the Christ of history. The gospel is based on historical facts and events confirmed by witnesses and recorded in the self-authenticating, inscripturated Word of God.

There are those who call themselves Christian teachers who tell us that the facts of what we find recorded in the Gospels do not matter that much. It is not important whether these things really happened, they say, but what matters is "the teaching" and "the religious value" of these stories and the personal experiences these stories grew out of in the early church and the experiences these stories evoke and produce in us. That's all that really matters.[1]

If there was ever a time in which we need to emphasize in our preaching the great facts and events in history on which the gospel is based and, indeed, are themselves the gospel, it is the time in which you and I are living. We must never forget that preaching the gospel is not a matter of engaging in philosophical speculations and theories. It is not a matter of advocating for a particular code of ethics or so-called traditional values. It is not even a matter of telling people about some wonderful experience you and others have had, though there's a place for that. It involves, first and foremost, the declaration of certain facts and events in history. Take away the historical facts and events, and you no longer have the gospel.

You may speak about your Christian experience to people, and that's fine and has its place. It is good to do that. But when you do it, the postmodern mind will say, "Great, that's wonderful. If that's the sort of thing that makes you happy, more power to you. If it works for you,

[1] Many of the thoughts contained in this and the next two paragraphs are adapted from the comments of D. Martyn Lloyd-Jones, *Studies in The Book of Acts, Vol 2: Courageous Christianity* (Wheaton, IL: Crossway, 2001), 164–165.

good. Personally, I'm not interested. I don't need it, but whatever works for you, go for it." Then we must also realize that cults can give people experiences. Dr. Phil, Oprah Winfrey, and various cults speak about getting happiness and peace and joy in your life: "Follow our advice, and you'll feel like a new person." Yes, psychology and the cults offer experiences, and they can sometimes give experiences. But the gospel we are called to proclaim is not merely about having wonderful experiences. It's about historical facts and events. We preach facts, historical events, concerning this person who is Lord of all and was sent by God to make peace between God and sinners. And we preach about what He has done in time and space to accomplish salvation. Without this person, and without those historical events, you don't have the gospel and you cannot be saved from sin and from eternal hell. Peter, therefore, sets forth the historical facts of the gospel.

He spoke of our Lord's earthly life and ministry. This One who is Lord of all humbled Himself and became a man. He came in time and space, and He lived in this sin-cursed world. Notice what Peter says in verse 37: "That word [that good news of peace] you know, which was proclaimed throughout all Judea, and began from Galilee after the baptism which John preached, how God anointed Jesus of Nazareth with the Holy Spirit and power." He speaks here of the beginning of our Lord's earthly ministry when He was baptized by John the Baptist in the Jordan River and the Spirit descended on Him like a dove. His human nature was anointed by the Spirit, equipping Him for His work as the God-man Messiah. Peter continues, "Who went about doing good and healing all who were oppressed by the devil, for God was with Him. And we are witnesses of all things which He did both in the land of the Jews and in Jerusalem" (v. 38–39). Peter speaks of Jesus's earthly life and ministry and how God was with Him attesting to and confirming His identity, as Jesus demonstrated His power over Satan, rescuing people who were in bondage to evil and tormented by demonic oppression. This is part of what is involved in preaching the gospel: telling about the life and ministry of the Lord Jesus.

Peter also declares of His curse-bearing death on the cross. Here we get to the very heart of the gospel, the end of verse 39: "whom they killed by hanging on a tree." The Lord of glory, the lovely, sinless Son of God, who went about doing good and nothing but good, was crucified on a cross. Again, Luke is only giving us a summary of Peter's message. In our preaching we must fill in from the rest of Scripture all that this death means. However, the meaning of His death is already alluded to right here in what Luke gives us. Notice the language: "whom they killed by hanging on a tree." "By hanging on a tree" is a shorthand reference to Deuteronomy 21:23. This text is referenced, or alluded to, several times in the New Testament, and it points to the curse-bearing nature of our Lord's death. There we read, "Cursed is everyone who hangs on a tree" (Gal. 3:13; see also Acts 5:30; 1 Peter 2:24).

The apostolic message of the cross may be viewed from different angles. The achievements of the cross are many. It propitiates divine wrath, it reconciles to God, it redeems from sin, it defeats Satan and frees us from his power. It accomplishes all these things and more for those who are trusting in Christ. But how exactly does it do this? What is the central focus and essence of the message of the cross? What exactly was happening to Jesus as He suffered and died? The answer given in the New Testament is that when Jesus died on the cross, He was offering Himself up as a substitutionary, curse-bearing sacrifice for sin. He was bearing the curse and wrath of God that we deserve for our sins as the sinner's substitute. This is the heart of the cross and the heart of the gospel. Though God is a God of love and mercy, He is also holy and just, and we, as sinners, deserve His wrath and eternal punishment for our sins. If in His sovereign grace and love God chooses to forgive sinners, it must be in a way that is righteous, in a way that upholds justice. How does God do that? How does God remain just and holy and yet freely forgive and justify sinners? Here is the answer that we must tell people and make clear to them. There is only one way. God put all the sins and all the guilt of those who will be saved to the account of His perfectly pure and sinless Son, and Jesus voluntarily received the punishment for those sins in the sinner's place. Indeed, God Himself was in Christ reconciling sinners to Himself. Think of it! God, in the person of the Son incarnate, bore the curse we deserve so that those who trust in Christ are freed from that curse and will never have to bear it.

> In this is love, not that we loved God, but that He loved us and sent His Son to be the propitiation for our sins.
>
> – 1 John 4:10

> Christ has redeemed us from the curse of the law, having become a curse for us.
>
> – Galatians 3:13

> Who Himself bore our sins in His own body on the tree.
>
> – 1 Peter 2:24

> *Death and the curse were in our cup;*
> *O Christ, 'twas full for Thee.*
> *But Thou hast drained the last dark drop—*
> *'Tis empty now for me.*[2]

Peter then proclaimed Christ's resurrection from the dead: "Him God raised up on the third day" (v. 40).

---

[2] Anne Ross Cousin, "Christ What Burdens Bow'd Thy Head," music by Ira D. Sankey.

Having borne the sinner's curse on the cross, Christ could not be held by the grave. If He had remained there, we could have. no assurance that our sins were effectively dealt with on the cross and we could have no hope after death. As Paul writes in 1 Corinthians 15:14, "If Christ is not risen, our faith is empty." But, praise God, "Up from the grave He arose, with a mighty triumph o'er His foes."[3] God raised Him from the dead on the third day. In this way, God was declaring and demonstrating that His Son's atonement was accepted and sufficient. Moreover, by His resurrection Jesus was vindicated in all His claims. Romans 1:4 states, "Declared to be the Son of God with power . . . by the resurrection from the dead."

Peter goes on to explain that Jesus's resurrection was physically verified by many witnesses. He says, "Him God raised up on the third day, and showed Him openly, not to all the people, but to witnesses chosen before by God" (Acts 10:40-41). That would include Peter and the apostles and over five hundred brethren, as Paul tells us in 1 Corinthians 15. And Peter makes it clear that Jesus was not a phantom; it was a literal bodily resurrection. Though His body was wonderfully transfigured and glorified, Peter says in the second half of verse 41 that they "ate and drank with Him after He arose from the dead." They saw Him, they spoke with Him, they touched Him, they ate and drank

[3] Robert Lowry, "Low in the Grace He Lay," music by Robert Lowry

with Him. Again, we see this emphasis on the historical Jesus.

Here we have the person of the gospel. We have the historical facts of the gospel, Christ's earthly life and ministry, His vicarious, curse-bearing death, and His victorious resurrection. This is preaching the gospel, telling the story of Jesus, who He is and what He has done. The old hymn says it well:

> *Tell me the story of Jesus.*
> *Write on my heart every word;*
>
> *Tell me the story most precious,*
> *sweetest that ever was heard.*
>
> *Tell how the angels, in chorus,*
> *sang as they welcomed His birth,*
>
> *"Glory to God in the highest!*
> *Peace and good tidings to earth."*
>
> *Fasting alone in the desert,*
> *Tell of the days that are past,*
>
> *How for our sins He was tempted,*
> *Yet was triumphant at last.*
>
> *Tell of the years of His labor,*
> *tell of the sorrow He bore*
>
> *He was despised and afflicted,*
> *homeless, rejected, and poor.*

Tell of the cross where they nailed Him,
writhing in anguish and pain;

Tell of the grave where they lay Him,
tell how He liveth again. [4]

3. The Urgency of the Gospel

In verse 42 Peter says, "And He commanded us to preach to the people, and to testify that it is He who was ordained by God to be Judge of the living and the dead." Peter is speaking of the last day when Christ will return to judge the world in righteousness. The living, those who are then alive on the earth, will stand before Him. And the dead, those throughout the centuries past who have already died, will, too, be raised to stand before Christ for judgment. What an awesome and solemn day that will be! Here Peter is making it clear, as we must also do in our evangelistic preaching, that the gospel is not just an interesting story for people to think about and consider. Eternal issues are at stake. The eternal destinies of men hang in the balance. Judgment is coming, and God has ordained Jesus Christ to be the judge.

And this Jesus Christ whom I declare to you, the Lord of all, the one who died for sinners and rose again, He will decide where you spend eternity. And what He decides then at that moment depends on what

---

[4] Fanny Crosby, "Tell Me the Story of Jesus," published 1880.

you decide now and how you respond to this gospel that I'm preaching to you.

And this leads me now in the next chapter to a third critical emphasis that must mark our preaching for conversions.

5

Pleading with Sinners

Peter in his preaching did not merely set before these people the facts of the gospel and their meaning and leave it at that. He never leaves it at that in any of his evangelistic sermons in the book of Acts. Every evangelistic message contains an earnest appeal. We see it here in Peter's sermon in the house of Cornelius: "To Him all the prophets witness that, through His name, whoever believes in Him will receive remission of sins" (Acts 10:43). In other words, my dear friends, here is the good news: Before you meet Jesus as Judge, you can meet Him now, today, as your Savior. Notice the language. There are two things I want us to see here. We have both the free offer and the immediate demand of the gospel.

The Free Offer of the Gospel

Peter preached the free offer of the gospel to all. "Through his name *whoever* believes in Him will receive remission of sins."[1] Whoever! The promise of the gospel is for all. Because of who Christ is and what He has done for sinners, *whoever* believes in Him will receive forgiveness of sins. It doesn't matter where you are from. It doesn't matter what you have done or how far down in the gutter of sin you may have gone. *Whoever* believes in Him will receive remission of sins—old, young, middle-aged, red, yellow, black, white. Open sinners, secret sinners, young sinners, old sinners, outwardly moral sinners, shamefully scandalous sinners— *whoever* believes in Him will receive remission of sins.

Forgiveness of sins is just one part of all the blessings that come to sinners who trust in Jesus Christ. It's the foundational blessing bringing with it all the others: justification, adoption into the family of God, the gift of the Holy Spirit who comes to indwell us and to sanctify us, and eternal glory and joy in the world to come. All these wonderful blessings of salvation should be set forth and explained, not necessarily each one in detail in every sermon but over the course of our evangelistic preaching. All this great salvation is freely given to *whoever* believes in Him.

Peter preached the free offer of the gospel to all, not only here but in his other sermons in the book of Acts. Acts

---

[1] Selected words are italicized by me for emphasis in the Scripture quotes in this chapter.

2:38: "Repent, *and let every one of you* be baptized in the name of Jesus Christ for the remission of sins; and you shall receive the gift of the Holy Spirit." Every one of you! Acts 3:26: "God, having raised up His Servant Jesus, sent Him *to bless you*"—to bless *you*—"in turning away *every one of you* from your iniquities."

And listen to Paul in Acts 13:38–39: "Therefore let it be known to you, brethren, that through this Man is preached *to you*"—to you personally, to you specifically, to you indiscriminately—"through this Man is preached *to you* the forgiveness of sins. And by Him *everyone* [*of you*] who believes is justified from all things from which you could not be justified by the law of Moses."

"*Whoever* believes in Him will receive remission of sins" (Acts 10:43). There are no limitations, no qualifications, no restrictions. None is excluded but those who exclude themselves by refusing to believe. Listen again to Paul in 2 Corinthians 5:20: "We are ambassadors for Christ, as though God were pleading through us, *we implore you* on Christ's behalf, be reconciled to God."[2] In the words of that great gospel invitation, Revelation 22:17, "*Whosoever desires, let him take* the water of life freely." Brothers, do you preach the free offer of the gospel?

---

[2] The word "you" is in italics in the English text and could just as well be translated "sinners" or "people."

Here, I'm afraid, is where some Reformed preachers struggle and hesitate and are lacking in their evangelistic preaching. "But wait a minute. We believe in the doctrine of election." By the way, Peter believed in the doctrine of election too. Just read his first epistle. Yes, we do believe in the doctrine of election as well as the doctrine of particular redemption, and rightly so, because the Bible teaches them. But we may be tempted to think that if God has already determined from eternity who will be saved, and if Christ specifically came to redeem all those the Father has purposed to save, then it's not proper to offer Christ and salvation to all. Or we may simply feel uncomfortable or uncertain doing so. How can we tell all who hear us that God sincerely offers Christ and salvation to them if God has not elected to save all?

The first answer is we must tell them this because the Bible tells them this, and thus, God tells us this. Granted, there's an element of mystery here. There's a tension here the Bible itself presents that my puny brain may struggle to reconcile. It's the tension between two dimensions of the one and perfect will of God. There is His will of purpose: what He has eternally purposed to do. And there is His will of precept: what He seriously and sincerely commands and calls on men to do.[3] But as one of the Puritans, I believe,

[3] This is also referred to as His will of decree, or decretive will, and His will of precept, or preceptive will.

put it, "Faith must swim where reason can only wade." It should not surprise us when talking about a glorious, eternal, and infinite God that there are dimensions of His being and His acts that are beyond our present and finite capacity to fully comprehend. And the same Bible that teaches the doctrine of election and the doctrine of a particular and definite atonement also teaches that God sincerely invites all men to come to Christ and promises to save them if they do.

It is a *free* offer. Isaiah 55:1: "Ho! Everyone who thirsts, come to the waters, and you who have no money, Come, buy, and eat. Yes, come, buy wine and milk without money and without price." Come receive this salvation; it is absolutely free. "Whoever desires, let him take the water of life *freely*" (Rev. 22:17). It is a *universal* offer. Isaiah 45:22: "Look to Me, and be saved, All you ends of the earth! For I am God, and there is no other." It is a *personal* offer: Forgiveness is preached *to you*; we implore *you*; the promise is *to you*.

And let me add, dear brothers, something notable. It is a *sincere* offer. It comes from the very heart of God. God sincerely extends His love to sinners in the gospel of Jesus Christ. He freely offers His Son and all the blessings of salvation that are in Him as a free gift, a free gift to be received by the empty hand of faith. Indeed, an offer that is not sincere and well-meant is not an offer at all. An insincere offer is a contradiction. As Sam Waldron writes,

"'Offer' contains in it the notion of a proposal presented to someone which the one presenting it desires for that person to accept."[4]

When I preach the gospel to sinners, is it proper for me to tell them that, in Christ, God is stretching out His hand to them in love and compassion and sincerely desires their salvation? The answer of the Bible is yes. It is true there is a special and eternal love God has for His elect. But does that mean God has no love of any kind for mankind in general or that in the gospel His saving love is not sincerely offered to them in Christ? John Calvin certainly didn't believe that. Commenting on John 3:16, he writes, "Even though there is nothing in the world worthy of God's favor, he shows himself gracious toward the whole world, and he invites all men without exception to faith in Christ."[5] On Ezekiel 18:23 Calvin says, "God desires nothing more earnestly than that those who were perishing and rushing to destruction should return into the way of safety. And for this reason, not only is the Gospel spread abroad in the

---

[4] Sam Waldron, *The Crux of the Free Offer of the Gospel* (Greenbriar, AR: Free Grace Press, 2019), 10. For anyone interested in delving deeper into the question of the free offer of the gospel and its consistency with the doctrines of sovereign grace, I highly recommend this work by Dr. Waldron.

[5] John Calvin, *Commentaries*, trans. and ed. J. Haroutunian and L.P. Smith, (Philadelphia: Westminster Press, 1958), 193–194.

world, but God wished to bear witness through all ages how inclined he is to pity."[6]

As mysterious and as difficult as it might be for our finite minds to comprehend and to reconcile with the doctrines of particular grace, the Bible does teach that in the free offer of Christ to all, God is sincere and that the invitations of the gospel are an expression of God's compassion for sinners as such. In Ezekiel 33:11 God swears by His own self-existence that He has no pleasure in the death of the wicked but sincerely desires that they repent and live: "'As I live,' says the Lord God, 'I have no pleasure in the death of the wicked, but that the wicked turn from his way and live. Turn, turn from your evil ways! For why should you die, O house of Israel?'" It is God who says, "Oh, that they had such a heart in them that they would fear Me and keep all My commandments, that it might be well with them, and with their children forever" (Deut. 5:29). Does that sound like a God who is not sincere? Is God just playing some kind of cynical game? No, see Him in the person of His Son, the God-man, weeping over Jerusalem: "O Jerusalem, Jerusalem, the one who kills the prophets, and stones those who are sent to her! How often I wanted to gather your children together, as a hen gathers her brood

---

[6] Calvin, *Commentaries on Ezekiel*, trans. Thomas Meyers (Grand Rapids: Eerdmans,), 2:246.

under her wings, but you were not willing!" (Luke 13:34).
I was willing, but you were not willing.

We are called to be like Christ; surely no one would
question that. But to be like Christ includes being
burdened for the salvation of sinners and feeling
compassion for sinners. We read in Matthew 9:36 that
"when He saw the multitudes, He was moved with
compassion for them." And feeling the difficulty of
reaching all those multitudes, He said, "Therefore pray the
Lord of the harvest to send out laborers into His harvest"
(9:38). In Luke 19 we read that "now as He drew near, He
saw the city [Jerusalem] and wept over it" (v. 41). And He
said, "If you had known, even you, especially in this your
day, the things that make for your peace! But now they are
hidden from your eyes" (v. 43). And He wept over the city.
And 1 John 2:6 says that "he who says he abides in Him
ought himself also to walk just as He walked."

We need to understand and be convinced that God is
sincere in His offers of mercy to sinners. If we're not, our
preaching will lack urgency and passion. We also need to
preach this to our hearers, for how can a man believe the
gospel and trust in Christ if he is not convinced that the
promises and invitation of the gospel are for him? if he is
not convinced that he is included and sincerely invited and
permitted now to believe the good news? if he is not
convinced that Christ, clothed in all His saving
accomplishments, is given to him by God to be his Savior

and stands ready and willing to save him? If you are not telling sinners that, you are not really preaching the gospel. And let me just say, you're not preaching like a true Calvinist either. It is a distortion of historic Calvinism that cannot or will not tell sinners this.

The reality of the well-meant offer is, in fact, embodied in the historic documents of mainstream Reformed faith. For example, the Canons of Dort (1618–1619) were written in part to state and defend the doctrines of Calvinism over and against the threat presented to the reformation churches of that time by the teaching of Jacob Arminius and his followers (Arminianism). However, while powerfully defending the doctrines of sovereign grace, the Canons of Dort also contain a clear affirmation of the sincere offer of the gospel to all. Under the Third and Fourth Heads of Doctrine, Article 8, it reads, "As many as are called by the gospel are *unfeignedly*[7] called. For God hath most earnestly and truly declared in His Word what will be acceptable to Him; namely, that all who are called, should comply with the invitation."[8] What about the Puritans? The Westminster Confession of Faith and her daughters the Savoy Declaration and the 1689 London Baptist Confession all speak in chapter 7 of each of "the covenant

---

[7] Italics mine. *Unfeignedly* means "sincerely."

[8] *The Three Forms of Unity: The Belgic Confession of Faith, The Heidelberg Catechism and The Canons of Dort* (Vestavia Hills, AL: Solid Ground Christian Books, 2012), 143.

of grace wherein he freely offereth unto sinners, life and salvation by Jesus Christ." Was it the Puritan understanding that God does so out of a heart of benevolent compassion for them? It was the great Puritan theologian John Owen, whose Reformed credentials are impeccable, to say the least, who wrote, "Love towards all mankind in general we acknowledge to be required of us" by the example of God's "own love and goodness, which are extended unto all."[9] Joel Beeke and Mark Jones give this quote from the Puritan Joseph Alleine as representative of Puritan preaching of the well-meant offer in *Puritan Theology: Doctrine for Life*: "The God that made you most graciously invites you. His most sweet and merciful nature invites you. O the kindness of God, his boundless compassion, his tender mercies."[10]

Iain Murray well argues that conviction of sin, though important and necessary, is not enough to woo and to wed the soul to Jesus Christ.[11] There is this suspicion common to fallen man that God is against him and unconcerned about his happiness. This suspicion must be removed, and it is only effectively and properly removed by the gospel. It is not removed just by the doctrine of the gospel but by

[9] John Owen, *The Works of John Owen* (Carlisle PA: Banner of Truth, 1976), 15:70.

[10] Quoted in Joel R. Beeke and Mark Jones, *A Puritan Theology: Doctrine for Life* (Grand Rapids: Reformation Heritage Books, 2012), 508.

[11] Murray, *The Old Evangelicalism*, 120.

faith in the declaration to that sinner that God extends His saving compassion and mercy *to you* in Jesus Christ and will most certainly save *whoever* believes on Him, *including you*. Murray quotes Bunyan on this point, "It is not the over-heavy load of sin but the discovery of mercy . . . that makes a man come to Jesus Christ." He also quotes the great Reformer John Knox, who said, "By what means Satan first drew mankind from the obedience of God, the Scripture doth witness: To wit, by pouring into their hearts that poison, that God did not love them." Part of the business of gospel preaching, according to Murray, is to extract that "poison" from the hearts of men.[12] But there's something else significant here.

The Immediate Demand of the Gospel

Peter not only preached the free offer of the gospel, he preached the immediate demand of the gospel. This gospel is for all, but the blessings of the gospel only become ours by believing in Jesus Christ. "Whoever *believes in Him* will receive remission of sins" (Acts 10:44). Here Peter mentions faith as the necessary response to the gospel, and elsewhere he mentions repentance—sometimes repentance and sometimes faith. The same is true of the preaching of Paul in the book of Acts. This is because whenever saving faith is mentioned in the New Testament,

[12] Murray, 120.

repentance is assumed, and when repentance is mentioned, faith is assumed. Repentance is the turning around of the whole life through faith in Christ as He is freely offered to us in the gospel. He came to rescue us from both sin's guilt and its domination over our lives. Likewise, faith in Christ is faith in Him to do just that; therefore, faith and repentance go together and are assumed in one another. Of course, the nature of faith and repentance and their relationship is something to be explained in our preaching. But the point I want us to see right now is that preaching for conversions involves not only pressing upon our hearers the universal offer of the gospel but also the immediate demand of the gospel: faith in the Lord Jesus Christ. The free offer of the gospel is not only a free offer, a universal offer, a personal offer, and a sincere offer, but it is also a *commanding* offer. It calls for an immediate response: "God . . . commands all men everywhere to repent" (Acts 17:30).

This is what we see in the examples of evangelistic preaching in the New Testament I just quoted from Paul's sermon to the men of Athens. Listen again to Peter in Acts 2:38 and following. After preaching the gospel, he calls his hearers to faith and repentance: "Repent and let everyone of you be baptized in the name of Jesus Christ for the remission of sins. . . . And with many other words he testified and exhorted them saying, 'Be saved from this perverse generation'" (vv. 38, 40). There is pleading; there are exhortations. He's urging them and calling them to repent and believe the gospel now, today. "Don't wait; don't go home and think about it. The gospel calls you to repentance and faith in Jesus Christ now before it's too late." Is there any pleading in your evangelistic sermons, brothers? When the Philippian jailer came to Paul and asked, "What must I do to be saved?" what did Paul say? "Sorry, you can do nothing; just wait on God and use the means and hope that He gives you faith"? No, he said, "Believe on the Lord Jesus Christ, and you shall be saved."

Let me quote from part of one of the sermons of the great eighteenth-century Calvinistic evangelist George Whitefield. This is from a sermon entitled "The Righteousness of Christ, An Everlasting Righteousness." Having expounded the text and opened the gospel, he goes to pleading with sinners. And this is typical of his evangelistic preaching.

> Come, dear souls, in all your rags; come, thou poor man; thou poor, distressed woman; you, who think God will never forgive you, and that your sins are too great to be forgiven: come, thou doubting creature, who are afraid thou wilt never get comfort; arise, take comfort, the Lord Jesus Christ, the Lord of life, the Lord of glory, calls for thee: through his righteousness there is hope for the chief of sinners, for the worst of creatures. What if thou hadst committed all the sins in the world? What if thou hadst committed the sins of a

thousand, what if thou hadst committed the sins of a million worlds? Christ's righteousness will cover, the blood of the Lord Jesus Christ will cleanse thee from the guilt of them all. Oh, let not one poor soul stand at a distance from the Savior. My dear friends, could my voice hold out, were my strength equal to my will, I would wrestle with you; I would strive with arguments, till you came and washed in this blood of the Lamb; till you came and accepted of this everlasting righteousness. O come, come! Now, since it is brought into the world by Christ, so, in the name, in the strength, and by the assistance of the great God, I bring it now to the pulpit; I now offer this righteousness, this free, this imputed, this everlasting righteousness, to all poor sinners who will accept of it. For God's sake accept it this night; you do not know but ye may die before tomorrow.[13]

My friend, is your preaching ever even remotely marked by earnest pleading and exhorting of sinners like that? Could it be we've become too formal, too dignified, too measured to preach in such a way? If so, may God have mercy on us.

This is something else I'm afraid some Reformed preachers may be missing in their evangelistic preaching.

---

[13] George Whitefield, "The Righteousness of Christ, An Everlasting Righteousness" in *George Whitefield's Sermons* (New Ipswich, NH: Pietan, 1993), 2:39.

Sometimes it's because of the fear of decisionism. But, brothers, calling sinners to faith is not the same as giving them some little canned sinner's prayer to pray after you and then pronouncing them saved because they did that. And it's not the same as calling them to move their body from one part of the church building to another during an altar call. Repentance and faith are spiritual acts of the soul, not physical acts. And the only calling on the Lord that saves is calling on Him with a heart that is, indeed, believing on Him (Rom. 10:13–14). But at the same time, faith is demanded of sinners in the gospel and demanded immediately.

Sometimes the hesitancy in preaching this way comes, again, from an imbalanced application of the doctrines of grace. This time it's the doctrine of total depravity and inability. We know that men are slaves to sin and unable to convert themselves. We know that no man will ever believe and repent unless God sovereignly imparts spiritual life to the heart of that dead sinner in regeneration. We know that. We also know that when God brings sinners to faith in Christ, it is His ordinary manner to do a prior work of awakening them to their sin and need, as we saw in our consideration of the preaching of John the Baptist. But here is the danger: making regeneration *the warrant* of faith in Christ. Or, if not regeneration, we can make preparation for Christ the warrant for faith in Christ. By *warrant* is meant that which makes faith in Christ permissible. But the warrant of faith is not regeneration or conviction of sin; it is not anything about the sinner or in the sinner. The warrant of faith is completely outside the sinner in the free invitation, promise, and command of God and the all-sufficiency of the Savior.

If we preach in such a way that our hearers get the impression that they have no warrant to come to Christ now, immediately, just as they are, or if we give the impression that there are some other qualifications they must meet or feelings they must have before they are invited and commanded to come to Christ and may safely venture upon Christ and be saved, we are promoting what is nothing more than a subtle form of works-righteousness. This will effectively keep them from *ever* coming to Christ. We are raising up roadblocks in the way to Christ. For how can I know I've been born again, or how can I know I've felt my need enough? You'll never know but by coming in faith to Jesus Christ, and if you do, you have. There's nothing else required, no prior qualifications. There's nothing you must do to make yourself fit. When we fail to preach the immediate demand of the gospel, we are also failing to confront the greatest of our hearer's sins, the sin of unbelief.

So, it's vital that we press upon our hearers the immediate duty to believe the good news. First John 3:23: "And *this is His commandment* that we should believe on the name of His Son Jesus Christ." What a wonderful command! God not only invites us to believe and be saved, He not only urges us and allures us with precious promises, He commands us to believe the good news and to receive the free gift of His Son to save us. And, praise God, it's always permissible to do what God commands and to do it immediately. You can never obey a command of God too soon. Indeed, we must make it clear when we preach the gospel that to do anything else short of believing, anything else but to comply with the gospel call, is to disobey God. Every one of your hearers needs to feel the weight of that. The gospel is not merely presented for our entertainment or information. Every soul who hears your gospel message that day will either walk away believing or continue in a state of rebellion against God, and there is no middle ground. If the sinner tries to excuse himself by saying he is unable to believe, he needs to be made to understand that his inability is a culpable inability, a moral inability. He cannot because his heart is so sinful and has such hard thoughts about God that he will not. And it's pressing this immediate duty to trust in Christ that God may use to expose to his view the wretched state of his sinfully resistant heart and bring him in the struggle to abandon himself to God's grace as his only hope. Or God might give that sinner faith right then and there as the gospel is being preached and you're calling him to Christ.

It may seem foolish to call on dead, blind sinners to repent and believe the gospel when you know all the while

they can't do it of their own power. You may be tempted
to say, "What's the point? Why call sinners to do what, by
nature, they have no heart to do?" But remember, the
gospel is the power of God to salvation. And it's often in
the very context of preaching the gospel in all its freeness,
as we set before our hearers the glory of Christ in His
person and His saving work, and as we call men to believe
and to trust in Him, that God in His sovereign mercy and
power grants them the grace to do so.

Think of the man with a withered hand in the gospels.
Christ looked at that man and said, "Stretch forth your
hand." But wait a minute, Jesus, don't you see, that's his
problem. His hand is shriveled; he can't stretch forth his
hand. But when Christ gave the command, in that same
instant He also gave him the faith and the power to obey
it. That's the romance, you might say, of preaching the
gospel. You never know what God will do in the hearts of
dead sinners as you stand and call them to faith in Jesus
Christ.

Think of Ezekiel's vision of the valley of dry bones in
Ezekiel 37. God set Ezekiel down in a valley full of bones,
and Ezekiel said, "And indeed they were very dry."

And God said, "Son of man, can these bones live?"

Ezekiel said, "O Lord God, you know."

And God said, "Ezekiel, prophesy to these bones and say to them, 'O dry bones, hear the word of the Lord!'" (vv. 2–4).

Now that sounds like a silly thing to do, to preach to dry bones. But Ezekiel didn't argue about it or try to figure it out. He did what God told him to do. And what happened? Ezekiel said, "So I prophesied as I was commanded, and as I prophesied, there was a noise, and suddenly a rattling; and the bones came together, bone to bone. . . . The sinews and the flesh came upon them, and the skin covered them over" (v. 7–8). And then God told him to prophesy to the wind and to call on the wind to blow on those bones, and Ezekiel says the "breath came into them, and they lived, and stood upon their feet, an exceedingly great army" (v. 10).

What a wonderful illustration of what God does through the preaching of the gospel. May God grant us the faith of Ezekiel. May He help us to believe in His power to save even through our feeble efforts.

I conclude this chapter with a paraphrase and adaptation of an excellent illustration given by Iain Murray.[14] Imagine there's a factory and a number of men who work at that factory. Within the factory there's a large, complex machine with many different wheels and pipes

[14] Murray, *The Old Evangelicalism*, 126.

and hooks and chains, which are interweaving and interlocking with one another. The workers are intended to operate this machinery. It's a complex machine, so complex that only the engineer who designed it can actually explain it and actually understands how all the parts work together and the relationship of each part. Only the engineer understands this; the workers don't. They're not even capable of understanding it. They're just ordinary men, some of them illiterate, who know nothing about the laws of mechanics or how the machine is designed and how it works. What if they decided that, because they can't fully understand how this machinery works, they're just going to sit and do nothing? How foolish that would be.

Well, dear readers, you may not fully understand how the divine machinery operates in the salvation of sinners, how it could be that God is absolutely sovereign in salvation and, at the same time, people are absolutely responsible and evangelism is absolutely necessary. But the fact is both are true. And instead of wearing yourself out with useless speculations and doing nothing, let us preach for conversions! Let us seek to awaken people to their lost condition and proclaim to them the glory and person and saving accomplishment of Jesus Christ. And let us press upon them the free offer and the immediate duty of the gospel to believe and be saved.

6

The Holy Spirit
and Preaching for Conversions

Now when the devil had ended every temptation, he departed from Him until an opportune time. Then Jesus returned in the power of the Spirit to Galilee, and news of Him went out through all the surrounding region. And He taught in their synagogues, being glorified by all. . . . "The Spirit of the LORD is upon Me, Because He has anointed Me To preach the gospel to the poor."

– Luke 4:13–15, 18

There is something critical for us to understand about the Lord Jesus Christ. In His state of humiliation, when He took to Himself human nature and entered this world to save us, He placed Himself wholly under submission to the Father's direction. As we read in Philippians 2:6–8, though He was equal with the Father and fully God, He "made Himself of no reputation, taking the form of a bondservant." And "He humbled Himself and became obedient to the point of death, even the death of the cross." He became obedient to whom? To the Father. And it was an obedience carried out in His true humanity by means of the indwelling presence of the Holy Spirit. He was also empowered by the Spirit to fulfill His ministry of preaching and teaching. The power of His preaching was the anointing of the Holy Spirit that rested on it and on Him. In fact, we don't find in the Gospels that Jesus ever opened His mouth in the public proclamation of God's Word until after His human nature was anointed for that work by the Holy Spirit at His baptism.[1] It wasn't until after the Holy Spirit descended on Him like a dove in His baptism and, being filled with the Holy Spirit, He was led by the Spirit into the wilderness to be tempted by the devil that, as Luke then tells us, "Jesus returned in the power of the Spirit to Galilee," and He began teaching in the synagogues (4:14–15). And in verse 18, He begins His sermon in the synagogue of His hometown, Nazareth, by quoting these words from Isaiah 61: "The Spirit of the LORD is upon Me, because He has anointed Me to preach the gospel."

This is one of the things that distinguished the teaching and preaching of Jesus from the scribes and Pharisees. A divine unction and authority rested on the Lord Jesus as He spoke. He preached in the power of the Holy Spirit.

Now, if it was necessary for Jesus to be filled with the Spirit and for His preaching to be empowered by the

---

[1] Albert N. Martin, *Preaching in the Holy Spirit* (Grand Rapids: Reformation Heritage Books, 2011), 9.

Spirit, how much more is that the case with ordinary preachers like us?[2] Indeed, this is absolutely essential to effective preaching. We preachers, in our efforts to preach for conversions, must have this to some real degree, or our preaching will never bear lasting fruit. Only the Holy Spirit can awaken and convince sinners of their lost condition. Only the Holy Spirit can regenerate sinners and give them the gift of faith and repentance. Only the Holy Spirit can make the Word of God effectual to convict and to convert the lost and to comfort and to build up and to sanctify the people of God. He does it through the Word. It's not the Spirit without the Word, and the Word alone can do nothing apart from the power of the Spirit giving life, illumination, faith, and penetration into the hearts of men.[3] Likewise, only the Holy Spirit can illuminate the mind of the preacher, giving him understanding in the Scriptures as he prepares his sermons, granting the certainty of faith in the truth he preaches and providing him fresh insights and timely words even as the sermon is being preached. Only the Holy Spirit can give to the preacher unfeigned urgency and passion and genuine love for Christ and for the people in the act of preaching. Without the power of

---

[2] Martin, *Preaching in the Holy Spirit*, 10.

[3] Stephen J. Lawson, "The Power of Jesus' Preaching: His Anointing by the Spirit," September 23, 2013, Sermon Audio.com, https://www.sermonaudio.com/sermoninfo.asp?SID=92313200259.

the Holy Spirit on a man's preaching, it will accomplish absolutely nothing of lasting value.

Now in the case of Jesus, a special empowering of the Spirit occurred at a specific place and time as a marked event in His life. It was at His baptism. It would be wrong to conclude from this that all gospel preachers must have an equally dramatic experience at a particular place and time. I believe that's saying more than Scripture allows. But there is a weighty truth here. Let us be clear about what we see in the example of our Lord Jesus. It is not that Jesus didn't have the Spirit in any way before this. No, what we see is that even Christ—conceived by the Holy Spirit in Mary's womb and upheld and filled with the Spirit with respect to His sinless humanity throughout the entirety of His life from His birth—received a special endowment of the Holy Spirit equipping Him for His public ministry and empowering Him to preach the gospel.[4]

We observe the same thing with the apostles later in the book of Acts. This is what Jesus promised to His disciples when He gave the Great Commission in Luke 24. He said to them, "Thus it is written, and thus it was necessary for the Christ to suffer and to rise from the dead the third day and that repentance and remission of sins should be preached in His name to all nations, beginning at

---

[4] Martin, *Preaching in the Holy Spirit*, 7–10.

Jerusalem. And you are witnesses of these things. Behold I send the Promise of My Father upon you; but tarry in the city of Jerusalem until you are endued with power from on high" (vv. 46—49). We read in Acts 1:8 that He said to them, "But you shall receive power when the Holy Spirit has come upon you." Power for what? "And you shall be witnesses to Me." Again, with the apostles a marked event occurred at a specific time and place when they received this special empowering of the Spirit for the first time. Granted, there's an element of uniqueness to their experience, which was tied to the peculiar significance of that one-time event of the initial coming of the Holy Spirit upon the new covenant church at Pentecost. However, there's still this underlying principle of the necessity of the power of the Holy Spirit in the ministry of preaching. And even after Pentecost, the apostles continually needed and received fresh infillings and empowerings of the Spirit in their preaching. It's not a once-and-for-all thing.

This book is not the place to give a full-blown exposition of the doctrine of the Holy Spirit. But let me just mention some basic facts. Every Christian is born of the Spirit and indwelled by the Spirit and sealed by the Spirit and baptized by the Spirit into the body of Christ. There is also a kind of habitual filling of the Spirit that is tied to our sanctification and that we are all commanded to cultivate and increase in (Eph. 5:18). But in addition to that, there is a special filling, an unction and empowering, for a specific task, which we also see in Scripture, including in the New Testament.

For example, in Acts 4 Peter and John are on trial before the Sanhedrin after the healing of the lame man at the temple. They were asked, "By what power or by what name have you done this?" (v. 7). We read in verse 8, "Then Peter, filled with the Holy Spirit, said to them . . ." But wait a minute. Wasn't Peter already baptized with the Holy Spirit at Pentecost? Yes, Peter was a man born of the Spirit, indwelled by the Spirit, and baptized by the Spirit, and he was living and walking in the Spirit. But this was a fresh empowering of the Spirit at that moment for that occasion. The gospel and the entire Christian church is standing on trial, and Peter needed power at that moment to witness effectively to the truth of Jesus Christ.[5] And right there and then he was given this fresh unction of the Holy Spirit.

Later in chapter 4 we read of the church now being threatened and persecuted and commanded to stop preaching. So they have a prayer meeting. This is the same church in Jerusalem but at a time well after Pentecost. And in response to their prayers, what happened? We're told they were filled with the Holy Spirit and spoke the word of

---

[5] D. Martyn Lloyd-Jones, *Preaching & Preachers* (Grand Rapids: Zondervan, 2011), 326. There is an excellent exposition of this subject and survey of the relevant texts by Lloyd-Jones on pp. 321–341 of this book that I found helpful.

God with boldness. They received this fresh filling and empowering of the Spirit to preach the Word. We continue to see this in the book of Acts. We see it with Stephen in Acts 7 and with Paul in Acts 13. We have these examples of this special enduement with power to speak the Word on specific occasions.

The apostle Paul, writing to the church in Corinth in 1 Corinthians 2:3–4, says, "I was with you in weakness, in fear and in much trembling. And my speech and my preaching were not with persuasive words of human wisdom, but in demonstration of the Spirit and of power." Again, there's this power in preaching given by the Holy Spirit.

Writing to the church in Thessalonica, Paul says in 1 Thessalonians 1:4–5, "Knowing, beloved brethren, your election by God." How did he know that? Did he climb up into the heavens and read some secret roll of the elect? No, he says, "Knowing, beloved brethren, your election by God. For our gospel did not come to you in word only, but also in power, and in the Holy Spirit and in much assurance." Two things Paul says about his preaching in Thessalonica: First of all, it came to them in words. He opened up and expounded and preached the gospel to them. Secondly, it did not come to them in word only. It also came in power and in the Holy Spirit. And how did he know that? He knew it because of what it produced in those who heard. They received the truth with much assurance. And as he goes on to say, "You turned to God from idols to serve the living and true God and to wait for His Son from heaven, whom He raised from the dead, even Jesus who delivers us from the wrath to come" (vv. 9–10). They heard Paul preach the Word, but that Word came accompanied by the power of the Holy Spirit producing faith in their hearts, resulting in their conversion.

Now this doesn't mean that every time the Word is preached in the power of the Holy Spirit everyone who hears will be converted. No, everyone who heard in Thessalonica wasn't converted. You can see that by reading Acts 17:1–9. Certainly, everyone who heard even Jesus preach did not embrace Him as their Savior and Lord. In fact, we see, in verses 28–30 of Luke 4, that the people who heard His sermon in the synagogue in Nazareth got angry with Him and tried to kill Him. The same was true with Paul's preaching. The point is not that Spirit-empowered preaching will convert everyone who hears it. Such preaching will be a savor of life to some and a savor of death to others (2 Cor. 2:16). But the point is this: Without the Spirit's power on our preaching, we have no reason to expect anyone to be converted. The power of the Holy Spirit—His power on both the preacher and the preaching—is essential to true preaching.

We could trace this out throughout the history of the church. In fact, this is what always happens in times of great reformation or revival. Ordinary men are given an extraordinary measure of the Spirit's unction upon their preaching. Read about Luther, Calvin, Knox; about the Puritans, men like William Perkins, Robert Bruce, John Livingston, and John Bunyan; about the awakening in the eighteenth century and the ministries of men like Jonathan Edwards and David Brainerd in America, George Whitefield and John Wesley and William Grimshaw and a host of others in England, Daniel Rowland and Howell Harris in Wales, James Robe and William McCulloch and others in Scotland. Preaching that results in conversions is preaching accompanied by the power of the Holy Spirit.

Now there are measures and degrees of this a man of God may know and experience, and we may know more of the Spirit's power upon our preaching at one time than another. As in all the works of God's Spirit, there's the ordinary, which we are not to despise, and there are those special times, the extraordinary, which are in the sovereign hand of God. But for our preaching to be lastingly effective to any degree and at any time, it must, in some measure, be accompanied by the unction and power of the Holy Spirit. To quote Spurgeon:

> To us as ministers the Holy Spirit is absolutely essential. Without Him our office is a mere name. We claim no priesthood over and above that which belongs to every child of God but we are successors of those, who in olden times were moved by God to declare his Word,

testify against transgression, and to lead his cause. Unless we have the Spirit of the prophets resting upon us, the mantle which we wear is nothing but a rough garment to deceive. . . . If we have not the Spirit which Jesus promised, we cannot perform the commission which Jesus gave.[6]

Brothers, may God help us to be convinced of how important this is. If Jesus, the Son of God Himself, in His perfect, sinless humanity needed the power of the Spirit in His preaching, how much more do we? So then, what should we do?

Well, this tells us that, first, we must be careful not to grieve the Holy Spirit in our lives. We must not tolerate and sign a truce with anything unholy in our lives. We must keep short sin accounts with God. We must be quick to repent when God convicts us of sin, quick to make it right and ask forgiveness if we become aware that we've sinned against another person, and in this way, maintaining a conscience void of offense toward God and toward others. This must be the way we live our lives day by day, walking in the light, humbly confessing our sins, pursuing holiness in the fear of God. We can't expect to enjoy the blessing of the Spirit upon our preaching if we are grieving the Spirit by a careless, unholy life.

[6] Spurgeon, *Lectures to My Students*, 2:3.

Furthermore, we must be men of the Word, filling our hearts with the truth and always growing in our study of the Scriptures. The Spirit and the Word work together. It is interesting that in Ephesians 5:18–19 Paul says, "And be not drunk with wine . . . but be filled with the Spirit, speaking to one another in psalms and hymns and spiritual songs." But in the parallel passage in Colossians 3:16, he says it this way: "Let the word of Christ dwell in you richly in all wisdom, teachings and admonishing one another in psalms and hymns and spiritual songs." We see that there is an implied connection, an intimate connection, between being filled with the Spirit and the word of Christ dwelling in us richly. A Spirit-filled preacher will always be a Bible-filled preacher. The man of God must be a man of the Word, feeding on God's Word for the nourishment of his own soul first. He must be a diligent reader and studier of the Scriptures. He must be always growing in his understanding of the Word. We can't preach truth we don't know. And we can't preach truth effectively, warmly, and boldly that we aren't certain of and convinced of ourselves.

We also need to live in daily believing, prayerful communion with the Lord Jesus, warming our hearts and feeding our faith on the wonderful promises of the gospel. And, brothers, we must also feel—and feel *deeply*—just how great our dependence on the Holy Spirit really is and continuously remind ourselves of this. We are dependent

114 Preaching for Conversions

on the Holy Spirit in our study and in our preparation of our sermons. We are dependent on the Holy Spirit in the delivery of our sermons. We are dependent on the Holy Spirit in the effects of our sermons on our hearers. We must be convinced of this. We must know and feel how helpless we are without the Spirit's power.

Furthermore, we must, with faith, seek this unction and pray for it. (I'll have more to say about that in the next chapter.) Better, we must seek *Him*.[7] Seek the Holy Spirit and His power on your life and on your preaching. Pray for this continually, persistently, and habitually. And, brothers, we can pray confidently and with faith, for God is not reluctant to give to His servants what we need to fulfill His calling on our lives.

There are exceptional measures of the Spirit's power at times. There are temporary and extraordinary seasons, and there is the ordinary in the gospel ministry. There are ebbs and flows, as it were. Also, there are various degrees of giftedness God gives to each of His servants. But with all those qualifications, if we are preachers of the gospel we must have the unction of the Spirit on our preaching. And God is able and willing to empower every one of us who is truly called to preach His Word insofar as we need to fulfill the particular ministry He has given to each of us. Let it not be said that we have not because we ask not (James

---

[7] Lloyd-Jones, *Preaching and Preachers*, 340.

4:2). Put your finger on our Lord's promise in Luke 11:13 and plead it before the throne of grace. Plead it and believe it as you prepare your messages and every time you preach, for "if you then being evil, know how to give good gifts to your children, how much more will your heavenly Father give the Holy Spirit to those who ask Him."

And, finally, there is something here we need to communicate to all God's people. One of the things you'll notice in the New Testament is that God's blessing on the preaching of His Word is not only to be a concern for the preacher. This blessing is often tied to the prayers of the church. I mentioned earlier in Acts 4 how the church came together and prayed that God would grant boldness to His servants to preach His Word. As they prayed, the place was shaken, and they were "all filled with the Holy Spirit, and they spoke the word of God with boldness. . . . And with great power the apostles gave witness to the resurrection of the Lord Jesus" (vv. 31, 33). There we see one of the characteristics of effective preaching: boldness, a confidence and assurance and certainty of faith and liberty of speech. We also see the agent by which this boldness in preaching is given: the Holy Spirit. They were filled with the Holy Spirit. And then we also see how this unction of the Spirit was obtained: the means of prayer. But in this case, not just the prayers of the preacher himself but the prayers of the people of God.

How often the apostle Paul asks the churches to pray for him concerning this very thing. Ephesians 6:19: "And pray for me, that utterance may be given to me, that I may open my mouth boldly to make known the mystery of the gospel." Colossians 4:3–4: "Meanwhile praying also for us, that God would open to us a door for the word, to speak the mystery of Christ . . . that I may make it manifest, as I ought to speak." You see, the people of God have a part when it comes to Spirit-empowered preaching in the church. Someone once asked Spurgeon, "Mr. Spurgeon, what is your secret?"—meaning, "What is the secret of your success?" Without hesitation he said, "My people pray for me."[8]

This leads us now to the subject of the final chapter of this book.

[8] Quoted by Iain Murray in *The Forgotten Spurgeon* (Carlisle, PA: Banner of Truth, 1986), 36n20.

7

Prayer and
Preaching for Conversions

Thus says the Lord GOD: "I will also let the house of Israel inquire of Me to do this for them: I will increase their men like a flock. Like a flock offered as holy sacrifices, like the flock at Jerusalem on its feast days, so shall the ruined cities be filled with flocks of men. Then they shall know that I am the LORD."

– Ezekiel 36:37–38

In 1747 Jonathan Edwards published a work entitled—and I'm just going to give you a shortened version of the title—*An Humble Attempt to Promote Explicit Agreement and Visible Union of God's People, in Extraordinary Prayer, for the Revival of Religion and the Advancement of Christ's Kingdom on the Earth.*[1] From now on we'll just call it *A Humble Attempt.* It was not the opening text on which the work is based, but one of the texts Edwards references in that work is Ezekiel

---

[1] Jonathan Edwards, *The Works of Jonathan Edwards* (Carlisle, PA: Banner of Truth, 1988), 2:278–312.

36:37. He also preached from this text to his own
congregation.

Later this treatise had a tremendous influence on
Calvinistic Baptists in England.[2] Around thirty-six years
later, in 1784, the Baptist pastor John Ryland received a
copy of *A Humble Attempt* from his Scottish friend John
Erskine. He was so moved by it he shared it with his two
Baptist pastor friends, Andrew Fuller and John Sutcliff.
Soon after reading it, these three men, together with a few
other ministerial colleagues, committed themselves to
meeting the second Tuesday in every other month to "seek
the revival of real religion, and the extension of Christ's
kingdom in the world."

A short time later, at the annual meeting of the
Northampton-shire Association, the proposal was made by
John Sutcliff that all the churches of the association
establish monthly prayer meetings for the outpouring of
the Holy Spirit and the revival of the churches in Great
Britain. The proposal met with wholehearted approval by
the representatives of the sixteen churches at the meeting.
He said:

---

[2] Much of the information in this paragraph and in the following
paragraph is adopted and adapted from Michael Haykin, *One Heart and
One Soul: John Sutcliff of Olney, His Friends* (Durham, UK: Evangelical
Press), 158–171.

The grand object in prayer is to be, that the Holy Spirit may be poured down on our ministries and churches, that sinners may be converted, the saints edified, the interest of religion revived, and the name of God glorified. At the same time remember, we trust you will not confine your requests to your own societies [i.e., churches], or to your own immediate connection [i.e., denomination]; let the whole interest of the gospel to the most distant parts of the habitable globe be the object of your most fervent requests. . . . Who can tell what the consequences of such an united effort in prayer may be! Let us plead with God the many gracious promises of his word, which relate to the future success of the gospel. He has said. . . [and here he quotes our opening Scripture], "I will yet for this be enquired of by the house of Israel, to do it for them, I will increase them with men like a flock" (Ez. 36:37).[3]

Let me add that through the ministries of men like Ryland, Fuller, and Sutcliff revival did, indeed, come to the Baptists. In 1750 the number of Calvinistic Baptist churches in England and Wales had dwindled to about 150. By 1794, ten years after the call to prayer and two years after the formation of the Baptist missionary society that sent William Carey to India, it's estimated that Calvinistic Baptists had increased to 326 churches in

[3] Quoted in Haykin, *One Heart and One Soul*, 164.

England and 56 in Wales, more than double the number in 1750. And just four years later, in 1798, the number was 361 in England and 84 in Wales.[4] John Rippon wrote, "It is said that more of our meeting houses have been enlarged within the last five years and built within the last fifteen, than had been built and enlarged for thirty years before."[5] And, of course, along with that was the formation of the mission society from which the gospel was to go forth to the heathen.

Again, one of the texts referenced in this call to prayer was the text at the head of this chapter. Now the question may be asked: Why did these men see this Old Testament text as supporting prayer for revival and evangelistic and missionary expansion in our day? Let me give something of the background of our text.

Ezekiel was among the people who were carried into Babylon prior to the destruction of Jerusalem. In chapters 1–30, his message is primarily a message of judgment. But after Jerusalem fell, Ezekiel's message in chapters 31–46 is primarily a message of hope. He speaks of the return from exile and the restoration of God's people. This is the primary reference and application in these latter chapters. However, as is often the case with the prophets, it's very clear, both in the scope and magnitude of what's

4 Haykin, 282.
5 Haykin, 282.

anticipated in these prophecies and in the use made of some of them in the New Testament, that they take in more than just the return from exile and the very small measure of blessing enjoyed in those days. The return from Babylonian exile was just a precursor and a pointer to something greater. They also point to what that event was preparing for: the coming of the Messiah and the establishment of the new covenant. Ezekiel prophesied in this section, for example, in 34:23–24: "I will establish one shepherd over them, and He shall feed them—My servant David. . . . I, the LORD will be their God, and My servant David a prince among them." He is talking about Christ. Then He says, "I will make a covenant of peace with them" (v. 25). Again, at the end of chapter 37, we read, "My servant David shall be their prince forever. Moreover, I will make a covenant of peace with them, and it shall be an everlasting covenant with them. . . . My tabernacle also shall be with them" (vv. 25–27).

Also, in the New Testament there are allusions to this chapter as finding a fulfillment in these gospel days. In Ezekiel 36:25–27, God says:

> Then I will sprinkle clean water on you, and you shall be clean; I will cleanse you from all your filthiness and from all your idols. I will give you a new heart and put a new spirit within you; I will take the heart of stone out of your flesh and give you a heart of flesh. I will put My

Spirit within you and cause you to walk in My statutes, and you will keep My judgments and do them.

You'll find these verses alluded to by the apostle Paul in 2 Corinthians 3 and in Romans 8. The apostles understood this as being fulfilled now in these new covenant days. Jesus Himself spoke of His death as the establishment of the new covenant.

My point is, these latter chapters of Ezekiel, though initially referring to Israel's return from Babylonian exile, take in much more than that. They speak in old covenant forms and pictures of spiritual blessings that are to mark this gospel age in which you and I live, the coming of the Messiah, and the establishment of a new covenant with a new and redeemed Israel, made up of both the believing remnant of the Jews and believing Gentiles. This is why our forefathers had no qualms taking a text like this and applying it to our present day and to the Christian church. Regardless of your eschatology, the principles here are timeless principles that apply to all God's people in every age, as I trust we'll see. With this in mind, let me try to open it up.

Great Blessings Promised and to Be Desired

In the previous verses, God is telling us what *He's* going to do. He's going to gather His people from among the nations (v. 24). He's going to do a work of regeneration and renewal in their hearts by the power of the Holy Spirit (vv. 25–27), which was referenced earlier. He then goes on to mention that He will give them security, prosperity, and fruitfulness in the land (vv. 28–30) and that He will give them the gift of repentance (vv. 31–32). "Then you will remember your evil ways and your deeds that were not good; and you will loathe yourselves in your own sight, for your iniquities and your abominations" (v. 31). He will cleanse them from all their iniquities (v. 33), and the land will no longer be barren and desolate (vv. 33–36). So, we have these promises of what God, in His sovereign mercy, is going to do, promises of regeneration and repentance, prosperity and fruitfulness.

And now, here in our opening text, God also promises multiplication. He says, beginning at the end of verse 37, "I will increase their men like a flock. Like a flock offered as holy sacrifices, like the flock at Jerusalem on its feast days, so shall the ruined cities be filled with flocks of men. Then they shall know that I am the LORD" (vv. 37–39). Here is a promise of multiplication, a promise of growth and increase and expansion. Really, we might call this a promise of spiritual awakening in old covenant language and in the context of new covenant promises. These are great blessings promised and to be desired.

Let's think a moment about this blessing of multiplication and increase in our text. "I will increase their men like a flock . . . the ruined cities will be filled with flocks of men." I trust we know that multiplication is set forth in Scripture as something good and as a sign of God's blessing. Often in the Old Testament this is so in a physical sense. Think of Genesis 1, after God created the man and the woman, we read, "Then God blessed them and God said to them, 'Be fruitful and multiply and fill the earth.'" Later, the same blessing is pronounced to Noah. This was also one of the blessings promised to Abraham: "Blessing I will bless you, and multiplying I will multiply your descendants as the stars of the heaven and as the sand which is on the seashore; and your descendants shall possess the gate of their enemies" (Gen. 22:17).[6]

Now this promise of the multiplication of Abraham's descendants has a physical fulfillment in the nation of Israel. But we also know it went beyond that to Abraham's spiritual descendants from among all nations who are blessed in Christ. As Paul writes in Galatians 3:29, "And if you are Christ's, then you are Abraham's seed, and heirs according to the promise." Multiplication is a blessing from God to be desired, and in this spiritual sense it is a great blessing for the church.[7] The lack of it is something to be greatly lamented and grieved over. It's something that ought to trouble us greatly.

[6] Charles Spurgeon, "Enquire of the Lord," *The Metropolitan Tabernacle Pulpit,* 22:504.
[7] Spurgeon, 22:504.

I trust we all realize this. I know there can be a lot of talk about church growth that's imbalanced and even foolish and unbiblical. In fact, isn't it true that often when we hear about a church that has a large congregation it's almost our reflex reaction to be a bit suspicious of that church? "Oh yeah, I wonder what they're doing to get people in—Super Bowl Sunday parties, decision-based altar calls, rockin' music, twenty-minute self-esteem sermonettes, no accountability or church discipline, and so on." We are immediately suspicious, aren't we? I think there is a sense in which we ought to be, knowing what we know about the climate of many American churches today. Large numbers are not always a sign of God's blessing. And it's also true that small numbers are not always a sign God is not with us. There are times when God's true people are a small and faithful remnant. However, in reacting against an approach to church growth that makes increasing numbers the ultimate end and any means that "works" to attract folks and to keep them entertained, we need to be careful. In reacting against a wrong kind of growth, we must not swing to the opposite extreme of not caring about growth at all or even priding ourselves in small numbers as a badge of orthodoxy instead of being alarmed about it.

One thing you will see when looking at the book of Acts is that Luke was into numbers. At the beginning of Acts, before Pentecost, he tells us the number of believers who were originally there in the upper room. He says, "Altogether the number of the names was about a hundred and twenty" (v. 15). Then in chapter 2, when Peter preached on the day of Pentecost, Luke tells us, "Then those who gladly received his word were baptized; and that day about three thousand souls were added to them" (v. 41). Then he goes on to say, "And the Lord added to the church daily those who were being saved" (v. 47). In chapter 4, verse 4, he says, "Many of those who heard the word believed; and the number of the men came to be about five thousand." You see, he speaks of multiplication as one of the signs of God's blessing on the church. And he continues to do this throughout the book of Acts. Acts 5:14: "And believers were increasingly added to the Lord, multitudes of both men and women." Then after deacons were appointed in Acts 6, he tells us, in verse 7, "Then the word of God spread, and the number of the disciples multiplied greatly in Jerusalem, and a great many of the priests were obedient to the faith." Acts 9:31: "Then the churches throughout Judea, Galilee, and Samaria had peace and were edified. And walking in the fear of the Lord and in the comfort of the Holy Spirit, they were multiplied." When the gospel first came to Antioch in chapter 11 we read, "And the hand of the Lord was with them, and a great number believed and turned to the Lord" (v. 21). And we continue to see references like this throughout the book of Acts. The multiplication of new converts and the growth and expansion of the church and the fruitfulness of the gospel are not mentioned in these passages as a bad thing but as a good thing, a wonderful thing, a glorious thing, a sign of spiritual health and vitality and of God's blessing on His church.

There is a proper sense in which we ought to be concerned about numbers. If it's the right kind of growth, if it is God adding to His church such as are truly being saved, I want to see that, don't you? How could you not want that if you're a Christian and—especially—if you're a minister of the gospel?

Verse 38 of Ezekiel 36 reads, "Like a flock offered as holy sacrifices, like the flock at Jerusalem on its feast days, so shall the ruined cities be filled with flocks of men." Note the next sentence: "Then they shall know that I am the LORD." Do you want men and women to know that the God we worship is the Lord? Do we want our neighbors, our lost family members, the people in our community, our nation, the world, the enemies of Christ who throughout our land are blaspheming His name, the movers and shakers of our culture who are leading us down the path of moral and cultural suicide, and those who raise their threatening voices against the church and God's truth to be shaken and arrested and caused to stand up and take notice? Do we want the mouths of the gainsayers who mock and laugh at the church to be stopped? Do we want them to be forced to confess that God is among His people of a truth and that there is, indeed, a God in heaven who saves sinners? Well, one of the ways that happens is when the Spirit is poured out and sinners are converted and the church is multiplied with the right kind of growth, when sinners are born again and truly converted and radically transformed by the grace and power of God.

The Means by which Such Blessing Is to Be Obtained

Not only do we have a great blessing promised to us but in verse 37 we have been told how such blessings are to be obtained: "Thus says the Lord, 'I will also let the house of Israel inquire of Me to do this for them.' " And for this reason, John Piper has rightly stated:

> Prayer is the coupling of primary and secondary causes. It is the splicing of our limp wire to the lightning bolt of heaven. How astonishing it is that God wills to do His work through people. It is doubly astonishing that He ordains to fulfill His plans by being asked to do so by us. God loves to bless His people. But even more He loves to do it in answer to prayer.[8]

Have you ever thought how God "ordains to fulfill His plans by being asked to do so by us?" Think about our text. Going back up to verse 24, repeatedly God has been telling

---

[8] John Piper, *Brothers, We Are Not Professionals: A Plea to Pastors for Radical Ministry* (Nashville: Broadman and Holman, 2002), 53.

us what He, in His absolute sovereignty and for His own glory, is going to do:

- ❧ "I will take you from among the nations" (v. 24).

- ❧ "I will sprinkle clean water on you, and you shall be clean" (v. 25).

- ❧ "I will give you a new heart and put a right spirit within you" (v. 26).

- ❧ "I will put my Spirit in you and cause you to walk in my statutes and keep my judgments" (v. 27).

- ❧ "I will deliver you from all your uncleanness" (v. 29).

- ❧ "I will increase their men like a flock" (v. 37).

I will do, I will do, I will do. But then He says, "I will also let the house of Israel enquire of Me to do this for them." In other words, "I will do it, but I will do it in answer to the prayers of My people. I will do it, but My people must pray and ask Me to do it."

This has been called the governing statute that regulates the increase of Christ's kingdom.[9] Over in that great Messianic psalm, Psalm 2, a psalm that speaks of the increase of Messiah's kingdom, we find that in a real sense even Jesus Christ Himself is subject to this divine statute

---

[9] I believe I heard it helpfully described this way, and the thoughts immediately following in the next three sentences, in a message or lecture by Al Martin many years ago.

regulating the increase of His kingdom. In Psalm 2:8 the Father says to the Son, "Ask of Me, and I will give You the nations for Your inheritance, and the ends of the earth for Your possession." Now, if Jesus Christ—co-eternal and co-equal with the Father in His Godhead, the God-man, exalted to the right hand of the Father in His kingly reign— must ask to receive what is promised to Him as the reward of His sufferings, then certainly it is the law of His kingdom that we, too, must ask if we would receive. It is not that God is reluctant to give. It is not that at all. But as John Piper has put it, "There is one thing God loves to do more than bless the world. He loves to bless the world in answer to prayer."[10] He has determined to carry out His purposes through the prayers of His people. I quote from Jonathan Edwards:

> It is God's will that the prayers of His saints should be one great and principal means of carrying on the designs of Christ's kingdom in the world. When God has very great things to accomplish in His church, it is His will that there should precede it the extraordinary prayers of His people, as is manifested in Ezek.xxxvi.37, "I will yet for this be inquired of by the house of Israel, to do it for them." And it is revealed that when God is about to do great things for His

[10] Piper, *Brothers, We Are Not Professionals*, 54.

church, He will begin by remarkably pouring out the spirit of grace and supplication (Zech. xii. 10).[11]

This has been the case throughout church history. An unusual spirit of prayer in the church is often a prelude to revival. David Brainerd put it this way when he wrote, "I saw how God had called his servants to prayer, and made them wrestle with him, when he designed to bestow any great mercy on his church."[12] This was true in the Old Testament, and the examples are many. And we see it in the New. What was the church doing before that first great outpouring of the Spirit on the day of Pentecost? Acts 1:14 reveals, "These all continued with one accord in prayer and supplication."

In Acts 4 the Spirit is poured out afresh on the same church, and what was the context? The church was in great danger, much like it is today in our country and in many places in the world. The powers that be were aligned against the church. They were determined to shut down its voice. There were the beginnings of persecution. The apostles were threatened and commanded to no longer preach or teach in the name of Jesus. What did they do?

[11] Jonathan Edwards, "Some Thoughts Concerning the Present Revival Of Religion in New England and the Way in Which It Ought to Be Acknowledged and Promoted," in *The Works of Jonathan Edwards*, (Carlisle, PA: Banner of Truth, 1987), 1:426.

[12] Quoted by Murray in a very helpful section on this subject in *Pentecost Today?: The Biblical Basis for Understanding Revival* (Carlisle, PA: Banner of Truth, 1998), 64–69.

We read that being let go, they went back to their companions and had a prayer meeting. They cried out to God for help and for boldness to preach His Word. And then we read in verse 31, "And when they had prayed, the place where they were assembled was shaken; and they were all filled with the Holy Spirit, and they spoke the word of God with boldness."

We could give other examples from the Bible, but let's think of church history. Take, for example, the evangelical awakening in England in the early eighteenth century. At least in part it was birthed out of prayer meetings that occurred in what was called the Fetter Lane Society. George Whitefield and the Wesleys and others were meeting regularly in 1738 after Whitefield returned from his trip to America. Whitefield tells us about these meetings:

> Sometimes whole nights were spent in prayer. Often have we been filled as with new wine. And often have we seen them overwhelmed with the Divine presence and crying out, "Will God indeed dwell with men upon earth! How dreadful is this place! This is none other than the house of God and the gate of Heaven."[13]

---

[13] Quoted in Arnold Dallimore, *George Whitefield: The life and times of the great evangelist of the 18th century revival* (Carlisle, PA: Banner of Truth, 1989), 1:221.

Are you aware of the amazing work of God that began in New York in the late 1850s?

Jeremiah Lanphier, a newly appointed city missionary to New York City, faced with the huge task of attempting to get people to church, decided to start a noon prayer meeting each Wednesday. He made and distributed a leaflet to offices and warehouses which invited workers to come to his North Dutch Reformed Church in Lower Manhattan to pray during the lunch hour from 12.00 noon till 1.00 p.m. They were welcome to come for five minutes—or else for a full hour. The door of the prayer meeting room was opened at noon on 23rd September 1857. Half an hour went by and no one came. Then, first one and then another came—six in all. These men prayed together. By October, as attendances increased, it was decided to hold these meetings daily. Within six months no fewer than ten thousand businessmen were gathering daily for prayer in New York. Within two years it is believed that one million professing converts were added to the American churches. This awakening shortly after passed over the Atlantic to Ulster, Scotland, England and Wales—then on, like a tide of blessing, to Australia, South Africa and South India. The number of converts is past all computation. This famous work of God began, at least in part, through a tiny prayer meeting.[14]

Extraordinary prayer is often the prelude to a spiritual awakening and an increased number of conversions. Or it might be argued that an unusual spirit of prayer is the beginning of such an awakening or one of the early marks of it. But either way, prayer and the conversion of sinners are ordinarily inseparable.

Many other examples could be given both from Scripture and from church history, all of which support the truth, in the words of Edwards, that "when God has very great things to accomplish in his church, it is his will that there should precede it the extraordinary prayers of his people."[15]

Why Is Prayer Connected to the Work of God?

What exactly is the connection between prayer and gospel work? Many answers could be given to that question. One is that God would have us pray to teach us and to remind us of our absolute dependence on Him. It's a lesson we so easily forget. But we must always remember, and we must be made to know it and to feel it, that the work God has

---

[14] Maurice Roberts, "Unction in Preaching" in *The Master's Trumpet*, published by the North American Presbytery of the Free Church of Scotland (Continuing), 2005.

[15] Edwards, *Works*, 1:426.

given us to do as preachers of the gospel is a work only God can make successful by His sovereign grace. We are called to labor and to work and to preach and to witness, yes, and with all our hearts. But we are laboring and working for that which only God can give. Success is not in our power or within our reach. Therefore, we must pray. Let's think about this.

In thinking about the conversion of sinners, do we really believe that unless God acts in power, all our efforts to preach the gospel will accomplish nothing? Do we really believe that? This is very powerfully illustrated for us by God Himself in the very next chapter, Ezekiel 37. There we have that great vision of a valley of dry bones we considered briefly back in chapter 5. God gives Ezekiel a vision of a valley of dry bones, a picture of Israel at that time, but it's just as much a picture of every lost sinner. Every time we stand up to preach, we are looking out over much the same scene. We see in the congregation many who are alive, but mixed in with them, sitting on the same row or even side by side, are some who are absolutely and completely dead, just as dead as those bones in Ezekiel's vision. There is absolutely no life in them, none. They are dead in trespasses and sins and doomed to eternal hell.

God says to Ezekiel, "Prophesy to these bones and say to them, 'O dry bones, hear the word of the Lord!' " (vv. 3–4). This is what we do whenever we preach the gospel, and this is what God commands us to do. We are preaching to dead people, dry bones, that cannot and will not and will never receive the message. They will never repent and believe because they are dead. But God tells us to preach to them.

Ezekiel does what God commanded him to do, and some things began to happen. Bone came together with bone, the skin came upon them, but still, "there was no breath in them" (v. 8). They were organized bones, pale, lifeless corpses; that's the best his preaching alone could do. They are still dead.

But then Ezekiel is told to prophesy to the *ruach*. The word for *wind*, *breath*, and *Spirit* in Hebrew is the same word: *ruach*. Cry for the breath, the wind, the Spirit. Ezekiel obeys and cries for the wind to come and to breathe on these dead corpses, and as he did, the breath came into them, and they were made alive.

Brothers, good preaching alone is not enough. We must cry for the Spirit to breathe upon the dead that they might live, for if He doesn't, they'll remain as dead as ever despite all our efforts. "I will also let the house of Israel inquire of me to do this for them" (Ezek. 36:37). Why? Because only God can do it. The case is desperate.

This is not only true when it comes to the conversion of our children and young people and of the people in our communities and of the millions still in darkness in the unreached parts of the world, it is true today with respect to the very continuance of the Christian church in our own land. That is always true, but there are times in which it seems especially true. There are certain times in the history of the church, or in the history of *a* church or a region or a country, when an awakening and an ingathering of souls is especially needed, and unless it comes, we're as good as finished. Brothers, it seems to me we're living in such a time in America and in Western culture at large. Our society is quickly spiraling into moral chaos. Christ is blasphemed. God's law is trampled underfoot. Good is called evil and evil is called good. Biblical morality, even common decency, is being turned completely upside down. And it's happening at breakneck speed right before our eyes.

This is the world our children are going to be living in, while many of them grow up in our pews, attend Sunday school, and sit under the preaching of God's Word and it seems to never move them. They grow up and move out of our homes, gospel hardened, while the churches in large part stand by and watch, completely powerless. Like the disciples at the bottom of the mount, when they sought to cast the demon out of the young man who had a mute spirit, and the young man's father said to Jesus, "Teacher, I brought my son, who has a mute spirit to your disciples that they might cast him out but they could not" (see Mark 9:17–18). What a picture of the church when the Spirit of God has, in large measure, withdrawn Himself. Do you remember what Jesus said to His disciples in that situation? They asked him privately, "[Lord,] why could we not cast it out?" (v. 28). And Jesus answered them, "This kind can come out by nothing but prayer and fasting" (v. 29).

Is God not calling His people to pray and to seek His face? Extraordinary, self-denying, sacrificial prayer is what is called for. May God not have to say of us, as He did of another generation, "There is no one who calls on [My] name, who stirs himself up to take hold of [Me]" (Isa. 64:7).

In What Manner Are We to Pray?

Of course, this is not just saying little prayers, mouthing words and repeating canned phrases then going on about our way. In the language of Isaiah 62:7, this is laying hold of God "and giving Him no rest till He . . . makes Jerusalem a praise in the earth." Let me just underscore three characteristics that need to mark our praying for conversions.

First, we must pray *repentantly*. What do I mean? Prayer is no excuse for disobedience. Let our prayers for conversions begin with this, "Search me, O God, and know my heart; Try me, and know my [thoughts]; and see if there is any wicked way in me" (Ps. 139:23–24). Let us begin by repenting of our sins, confessing our sins of complacency and self-dependence, acknowledging our pride in trusting in ourselves and thinking that if we just have the right doctrine and follow the right practice, all is well. We should reflect on how we ourselves have contributed by our sins to the barrenness of the church and to the degradation of our culture. Are we innocent in all this, my friends? Have we not contributed to the downgrade? Have we not contributed by our prayer-lessness, by our many compromises? Have you been allowing yourself in those little sins that eat away at your spiritual strength, those little sins that damage your testimony before the world? What about the way we live before our families? What about what you watch for entertainment? What are you looking at on your computer or on your cell phone? What about the secret place, the prayer closet, your Bible? Judgment must begin with us who are called to be ministers of the gospel. If we're going to pray for conversions, we must not pray as a substitute for obedience or as a cover for hypocrisy.

Second, let us pray *persistently*. Sometimes God gives His children exactly what they ask for at the very time they ask it. But often, for His own wise reasons, He requires us to be persistent. We see it in the story of Jacob wrestling with God at the brook Jabbok. The Angel of Jehovah says to Jacob, " 'Let me go, for the day breaks.' But [Jacob] said, 'I will not let You go unless You bless me!' " (Gen. 32:26). God acts as if He would leave, but He was testing and developing Jacob's faith. Jacob persisted, would not let Him go, and his prayer was answered.

Remember the poor Canaanite woman. Oh, how she cried, "Have mercy on me, O Lord, Son of David" (Matt. 15:22). But Jesus "answered her not a word" (v. 23). Again, and again she cried, and there was still no answer. The disciples tried to send her away, but she kept on. She cried, she followed Him, she ignored His seeming rebuffs and the rebukes of His disciples, she fell at His feet, she worshiped Him. She kept on and would not give up until finally Jesus said to her, "O woman, great is your faith! Let it be as you desire" (v. 30).

What are these examples and others like them in Scripture intended to teach us? Are they intended to show us that God is reluctant to bless His people? No, they teach us that we must continue to seek God and be persistent. We are not to be easily put off. We are called to importunity. God would sometimes prove and develop our faith by the process. He would teach us truly to value as we ought what we are seeking from Him by not giving it to us immediately. And in all this He is conditioning His people to receive the blessing properly in His good time. So we must pray persistently.

Third, and finally, let us pray *expectantly*. But do we have a promise in the Bible that God will bring conversions if we pray for them? We must acknowledge that conversion is a sovereign work of God. God chooses who, when, and where with reference to even just one conversion. But at the same time, the Scriptures abound with encouragements for us to pray for fruitful seasons from the hand of the Lord and, as we pray, to look for them expectantly. There are passages like the one with which this chapter was opened. In fact, the most common prayers you'll find in the Bible are prayers for restoration and revival and spiritual awakening. These prayers are recorded for future generations, for the church. God Himself has drawn up the petitions and has put them into our mouths:

> Our soul is bowed down to the dust. . . . Arise for our help, and redeem us for Your mercies' sake.
>
> – Psalm 44:25–26

> Return, we beseech You, O God of hosts; Look down from heaven and see, and visit this vine. . . . Revive us, and we will call upon Your name. Restore us, O Lord God of hosts! Cause Your face to shine, and we shall be saved.
>
> – Psalm 80:14, 18–19

We could go on with one prayer after another like this that teaches us how to pray and what to pray for.

Then there are the great prayers in Paul's epistles for the churches to know more of the Spirit's power. For example, Ephesians 3:14–16: "For this reason I bow my knees to the Father of our Lord Jesus Christ, from whom the whole family in heaven and earth is named, that He would grant you, according to the riches of His glory, to be strengthened with might through His Spirit in the inner man." This is a biblical prayer.

There is the first half of the Lord's Prayer: "Hallowed be Your name. Your kingdom come. Your will be done on earth as it is in heaven" (Luke 11:12). And how does that happen? It happens when sinners are being converted and the church is prospering and bearing fruit and the gospel is being sent out to the nations.

And if we will notice, these are not just prayers, they are promises:

> The poor and needy seek water, but there is none,
> Their tongues fail for thirst.
> I, the LORD, will hear them;
> I, the God of Israel will not forsake them.
> I will open rivers in desolate heights,
> And fountains in the midst of the valleys;
> I will make the wilderness a pool of water,
> And the dry land springs of water. (Isa. 41:17–18)

Consider that great promise of the Lord Jesus: Ask and seek and knock, for "if you then, being evil, know how to give good gifts to your children, how much more will your heavenly Father give the Holy Spirit to those who ask Him!" (Luke 11:13).

Brothers, let us pray expectantly. Let us acquaint ourselves with God's great works in the past and remember that He is a God who never changes. Remember, He is a

God who is graciously well-disposed toward His people. He has demonstrated it by giving us His very own Son to redeem us. And in the cross, He has made the way in which He can show mercy—mercy to men, women, and children who do not deserve it but deserve just the opposite—without in any way compromising His justice. Judgment is His "strange work," says the prophet (Isa. 28:21 KJV). He is a God who is slow to anger and abounding in mercy. "He will not always strive with us, nor will He keep His anger forever" (Ps. 103:9).

Let us pray, let us pray privately, let us pray in our families, let us pray together in small groups. And dear preacher and pastor, keep up the prayer meeting in your church. I urge you to keep up the prayer meeting. If you do not have one, start one. Make the prayer meeting an uncompromised, nonnegotiable priority in the life of your church. Urge your people to be there and teach them why it's so important.

May God grant us conversions—true conversions. And may Christ be glorified in our ministries, in our churches, and throughout the world!

On Campus & Distance Options Available

GRACE BIBLE
THEOLOGICAL
SEMINARY

Interested in becoming a student
or supporting our ministry?
Please visit gbtseminary.org